Praise for
Two Gentlemen of Lebowski

"Adam Bertocci has done a stellar job fusing the spirit of Shakespeare with *The Big Lebowski*. This mashup is one for the ages."
—Scott Shuffitt, cofounding Dude of Lebowski Fest
and coauthor of *I'm a Lebowski, You're a Lebowski*

"A blast to read."
—Zach Dionne, *GQ*

"Oh my God . . . This is so good." —Jonathan Chait, *The New Republic*

"Classic lines and scenes now become even more epic."
—Whitney Matheson, *USA Today*

"The mash-up that toke its time in coming." —*Time Out New York*

"Gadzooks, methinks 'tis all as fine a way to waste an hour or so as I have come across in these four seasons."
—Clark Collis, *Entertainment Weekly*

"Written by the incredibly talented Adam Bertocci, it is arguably one of the most inventive pieces ever created." —Broadway World

"Brilliantly crafted . . . *Two Gentlemen of Lebowski* proves that Shakespearean sharp-tongued eloquence is nifty even in the 21st century."
—Marina Galperina, Inside New York

"It's wonderful." —*Metro* (UK)

"Should be quite the what-have-you." —Gothamist

"It's the greatest thing since Geoffrey Chaucer." —Cinematical

"We were totally blown away to discover . . . this Swiss fucking watch of a genius named Adam Bertocci. . . . Verily, *Two Gentlemen of Lebowski* has to be read to be believed. Zounds!"
—The Dudespaper ("A Lifestyle Magazine for the Deeply Casual")

"Even those of us new to the Dude have become true believers in the Knave." —Lauren Wissot, TheaterOnline

"Bertocci's writing is solid, clever, and witty." —Boston Lowbrow

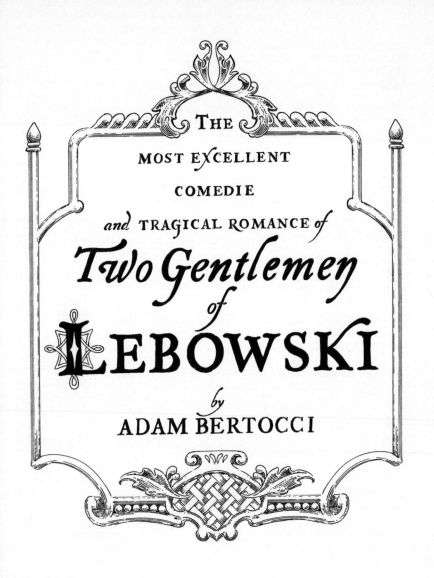

THE
MOST EXCELLENT
COMEDIE
and TRAGICAL ROMANCE *of*

Two Gentlemen
of
LEBOWSKI

by
ADAM BERTOCCI

Simon & Schuster Paperbacks
New York London Toronto Sydney

Simon & Schuster Paperbacks
A Division of Simon & Schuster, Inc.
1230 Avenue of the Americas
New York, NY 10020

First Simon & Schuster trade paperback edition October 2010

SIMON & SCHUSTER PAPERBACKS and colophon are registered trademarks of Simon & Schuster, Inc.

For information about special discounts for bulk purchases,
please contact Simon & Schuster Special Sales at 1-866-506-1949
or business@simonandschuster.com.

The Simon & Schuster Speakers Bureau can bring authors to your live event.
For more informaiton or to book an event contact the Simon & Schuster Speakers Bureau at 1-866-248-3049 or visit our website at www.simonspeakers.com.

Designed by Nancy Singer

Manufactured in the United States of America

10 9 8 7 6 5 4 3 2 1

Library of Congress Cataloging-in-Publication Data
Bertocci, Adam.
    Two gentlemen of Lebowski : a most excellent comedie and tragical romance /
Adam Bertocci. — 1st Simon & Schuster trade paperpack ed.
        p. cm.
    I. Shakespeare, William, 1564–1616. Two gentlemen of Verona.
    II. Big Lebowski (Motion picture)   III. Title.
    PS3602.E7684T96 2010
    812'.6—dc22   2010031819

ISBN 978-1-4516-0581-5
ISBN 978-1-4516-0583-9 (ebook)

For Richard and Danielle Bertocci,
from their little achiever

Two Gentlemen of LEBOWSKI

The Persons of the Play

CHORUS

GEOFFREY 'THE KNAVE' LEBOWSKI

BLANCHE ⎱ thugs
WOO ⎰

SIR WALTER of Poland

SIR DONALD of Greece

BRANDT, serving-man of the Big Lebowski

SIR GEOFFREY OF LEBOWSKI, the Big Lebowski

BONNIE, wife to the Big Lebowski

OLIVER, consort to Bonnie

JACK SMOKE, a cavalier

JOSHUA QUINCE, a paederast

LIAM O'BRIEN, partner of Joshua Quince

MAUDE, daughter of the Big Lebowski

VARLETS, employed by Maude

Two NIHILISTS

PLAYER QUEEN

MISTRESS QUICKLY, hostess of a tavern

KNOX HARRINGTON, a tapestry artist

DOCTOR BUTTS, a physician

PLAYERS for a dance

LAURENCE SELLERS

CLOWN

JAQUES TREEHORN

BROTHER SEAMUS, an Irish monk

GRAVEDIGGER

TWO GENTLEMEN
OF
LEBOWSKI

ACT I

Chorus: a character who provides exposition and commentary. The role originated in ancient Greek drama.

4 **kin:** family

5 **knave:** a man of humble birth or position; a roguish chap; other meanings include 'fellow' or 'boy.' The word derives from the Old English *cnafa*.

6 **bowl:** to play at a game of bowls. Such games were popular in Shakespeare's time, though often negatively compared with the more noble sport of archery. The verb dates to the 1530s.

9 **homelands mine:** unknown. Some scholars pin this play's Chorus as out of Western England; others, merely far from Eastern.

11 **arid vale:** dry valley

19 **fair Albion:** beautiful Great Britain. The name stems from the striking white cliffs of Dover (Latin *alba*, white).

20 **bawdy songs:** lyrical ribaldry. Other examples of the period include Stefano's song in *The Tempest*, Chaucer's 'The Miller's Tale,' John Isham's 'When Celia Was Learning on the Spinet to Play' and the unattributed 'The Comical Wager, being an Account of a Lawyer's Wife who laid a Guinea with her Husband's Clerk, that he did not Flourish her Seven times in an Hour.'

Fair Albion.

PROLOGUE

Enter CHORUS.

CHORUS
In wayfarer's worlds out west was once a man,
A man I come not to bury, but to praise.
His name was Geoffrey Lebowski call'd, yet
Not called, excepting by his kin.
That which we call a knave by any other name   5
Might bowl just as sweet. Lebowski, then,
Did call himself 'the Knave', a name that I,
Your humble chorus, would not self-apply
In homelands mine; but, then, this Knave was one
From whom sense was a burden to extract,   10
And of the arid vale in which he dwelt,
Also dislike in sensibility;
Mayhap the very search for sense reveals
The reason it inspires me to odes.
(In couplets first, and then a sonnet brave   15
As prologue to the tale of this the Knave.
Behold him, then, a-tumbling soft in sand
To pledge his love immortal to the land.)
We stray now from fair Albion and from France
And see no Queen of bawdy songs and cheers   20
And in an angel's city take our chance

23 **Arab kings:** Shakespeare refers to the Arabian King Malchus in *Antony and Cleopatra*, but this is a wild guess until we are privy to new historical discoveries

28 **god Olympian:** one of the twelve principal deities of Greek mythology, who resided atop Mount Olympus and ruled over the known world and beyond, perhaps even up to Pismo. The group was also called the 'Dodekatheon.'

31 **sloth:** indolence and world-class aversion to work. One of the seven deadly sins.

A theatre.

For stupefying tales to take our ears.
To war on Arab kings acoast we go,
Needing a man of times, though hero not;
Hear me call him not hero; what's in a hero?   25
Sometimes there's a man, your prologue's thought.
The Knave, though scarcely man of honour'd grace,
Nor god Olympian, nor yet employ'd,
Was nonetheless for all his time and place,
The man befits the circle he's enjoy'd.   30
A man of lazy ways, of epic sloth;
But, losing train of thought, I've spake enough!

Exits.

4 **forgive thee:** i.e., forgive the debt, cancel the claim

5 **chamber-pot:** a vessel used for urination and defecation. In Shakespeare's *Coriolanus*, Menenius upbraids the Roman tribunes for their immaturity, comparing them to overacting pantomime performers stricken with colic and 'roaring for a chamber-pot.'

9 **ducats:** gold coins of European origin. Shakespeare was rather free with the specific value of money, with a single ducat varying in worth.

A chamber-pot.

ACT 1

SCENE 1

THE KNAVE's house. Enter THE KNAVE, carrying parcels, and BLANCHE and WOO. They fight.

BLANCHE
Whither the money, Lebowski? Faith, we are as servants to Bonnie; promised by the lady good that thou in turn were good for't.

WOO
Bound in honour, we must have our bond; cursed be our tribe if we forgive thee.

BLANCHE
Let us soak him in the chamber-pot, so as to turn his head. 5

WOO
Aye, and see what vapourises; then he will see what is foul.

They insert his head into the chamber-pot.

BLANCHE
What dreadful noise of waters in thine ears! Thou hast cool'd thy head; think now upon drier matters.

WOO
Speak now on ducats else again we'll thee duckest; whither the money, Lebowski? 10

13 **rash egg:** impolitically bold child or spawn. 'Egg' also calls to mind 'zero' (as in the French *l'oeuf)* and hints at the thugs' unimpressed reaction to the Knave's dwelling.

20 **deadbeat:** a person who evades the payment of, or defaults on, a debt

THE KNAVE
Faith, it awaits down there someplace; prithee let me glimpse
again.

WOO
What, thou rash egg! Thus will we drown thine exclamations.

They again insert his head into the chamber-pot.

BLANCHE
Trifle not with the fury of two desperate men. Long has thy
wife sealed a bond with Jaques Treehorn; as blood is to blood,   15
surely thou owest to Jaques Treehorn in recompense.

WOO
Rise, and speak wisely, man—but hark;
I see thy rug, as woven i'the Orient,
A treasure from abroad. I like it not.
I'll stain it thus; to deadbeats ever thus.   20

He stains the rug.

THE KNAVE
Sir, prithee nay!

BLANCHE
Now thou seest what happens, Lebowski, when the agreements
of honourable business stand compromised. If thou wouldst
treat money as water, flowing as the gentle rain from heaven,
why, then thou knowest water begets water; it will be a watery   25
grave your rug, drown'd in the weeping brook. Pray remember,
Lebowski.

33 **profanes:** debases, defiles, corrupts

35 **Geoffrey, the married man:** Elizabethan mores viewed bachelor-hood with suspicion. Men were expected to be married, and often had to be to accept public office or important civic responsibilities.

37 **baldric:** a belt or sash worn over the shoulder

39 **lid of my chamber-pot:** a lid is customarily placed upon the pot to contain odours. Leaving it off indicates the Knave's incivility and lack of a wife.

43 **confounded:** perplexed. Blanche means 'confounding,' though that is not the issue here.

43 **orb:** sphere

44 **ninepins:** the sport of kings. Variants and alternate names include loggats, kayles, and skittles. Shakespeare frequently referred to the sport: in *The Taming of the Shrew,* it is a metaphor for Petruchio's courtship of Katherine; in *Coriolanus,* Menenius compares his over-committed loyalty to the title character to a poorly rolled frame; and, most famously, Hamlet's line 'Ay, there's the rub' refers to an obstacle deflecting a bowling ball from its course.

45 **colfer:** a player of 'colf,' the Dutch predecessor to the Scottish game of golf. In the sixteenth century, as the modern game filtered down from Scotland, its variants were enjoyed by commoners and royalty alike; Mary, Queen of Scots, was an avid golfer.

46 **varlet:** a rascal or disreputable character, from the Old French *vaslet*

An orb.

THE KNAVE
Thou err'st; no man calls me Lebowski. Hear rightly, man!—for
thou hast got the wrong man. I am the Knave, man; Knave in
nature as in name.　　　　　　　　　　　　　　　　　30

BLANCHE
Thy name is Lebowski. Thy wife is Bonnie.

THE KNAVE
Zounds, man. Look at these unworthiest hands; no gaudy gold
profanes my little hand. I have no honour to contain the ring. I
am a bachelor in a wilderness. Behold this place; are these the
towers where one may glimpse Geoffrey, the married man? Is　35
this a court where mistresses of common sense are hid? Not for
me to hang my bugle in an invisible baldric, sir; I am loath to
take a wife, or she to take me until men be made of some other
mettle than earth. Hark, the lid of my chamber-pot be lifted!

WOO
Search his satchel! His words are a fantastical banquet to work　40
pell-mell havoc and confusion upon his enemies. There sits
eight pounds of proof within.

BLANCHE
Villainy! Why this confounded orb, such as men use to play at
ninepins; what devilry, these holes in holy trinity?

THE KNAVE
Obviously thou art not a colfer.　　　　　　　　　　　45

BLANCHE
Then thou art a man to carry ball in his sack? Thou varlet, a
plague upon your house; I return thine orb to earth.

50 **of droplets:** i.e., only has a little urine left. Possibly a reference to the use of the aspergillum to sprinkle holy water in religious ceremonies, as if Woo is blessing the rug.

52 **chalcedony:** a fine mineral, similar to quartz. Named for the Bithynian port town of Chalcedon.

57 **house-broken:** versed in sanitary excretory habits suitable for civilised living; in casual speech, meaning docile or peaceably mannered.

Exeunt: they exit

severally: separately

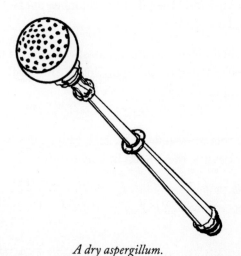

A dry aspergillum.

He drops the ball.

Thy floor cracks in haste, sir; thou art not a man of ample foundation. Woo?

WOO
Speak, friend; I am but of droplets.   50

BLANCHE
Was this not a man of moneys and repute? Did not Treehorn speak of chalcedony halls, and three chests of gold, as was hard food for Midas? What think'st thou?

WOO
O undistinguish'd man! We are deceived; this man has put not money in his purse.   55

THE KNAVE
Weep not for grief of my own sustaining, sir. At least I am house-broken, none to break the houses of others.

WOO
If dog you are, in time you'll have your day;
Waste time, but Jaques Treehorn will you pay.

Exeunt severally.

SCENE 2

The bowling green. Enter THE KNAVE, WALTER, and DONALD, to play at ninepins.

WALTER
In sooth, then, faithful friend, this was a rug of value? Thou wouldst call it not a rug among ordinary rugs, but a rug of pur-

4 **Whitsun:** Pentecost; from 'White Sun,' the seventh Sunday after Easter. This feast commemorates the descent of the Holy Spirit upon Christ's apostles. Morris-dancing figured heavily in celebrations of Pentecost.

4 **morris-dance:** an English folk dance that often incorporates handkerchiefs or other waved props. Shakespearean actor Will Kempe famously morris-danced from London to Norwich in nine days.

7 **scythe:** an agricultural tool used to reap crops and/or souls

10 **geometer's cap:** the ceremonial headwear earned by dint of effort and high achievement in the field of spatial mathematics

14 **unhappy:** unfortunate

18 **attend:** pay attention to

21–22 **groundlings:** the lowest tier of theatregoers in Shakespeare's day, socially, financially, and geographically. The price for standing-room-only seats below the stage was one penny.

Morris-dancing.

pose? A star in a firmament, in step with the fashion alike to the Whitsun morris-dance? A worthy rug, a rug of consequence, sir?

THE KNAVE
It was of consequence, I should think; verily, it tied the room 5
together, gather'd its qualities as the sweet lovers' spring grass
doth the morning dew or the rough scythe the first of autumn
harvests. It sat between the four sides of the room, making
substance of a square, respecting each wall in equal harmony,
in geometer's cap; a great reckoning in a little room. Verily, it 10
transform'd the room from the space between four walls pre-
sented, to the harbour of a man's monarchy.

WALTER
Indeed, a rug of value; an estimable rug, an honour'd rug; O
unhappy rug, that should live to cover such days!

DONALD
Of what dost thou speak, that tied the room together, Knave? 15
Take pains, for I would well hear of that which tied the room
together.

WALTER
Didst thou attend the Knave's tragic history, Sir Donald?

DONALD
Nay, good Sir Walter, I was a-bowling.

WALTER
Thou attend'st not; and so thou hast no frame of reference. Thou 20
art as a child, wandering and strutting amidst the groundlings as a play is in session, heeding not the poor players, their
exits and their entrances, and, wanting to know the subject of
the story, asking which is the lover and which the tyrant.

27 **bower:** a shaded refuge

29 **fulcrum:** support for a lever; from the Latin *fulcire,* to prop

31 **toughs:** hoodlums, ruffians of the common street

35 **aggression uncheck'd:** possibly a reference to a lost early draft of
Queen Elizabeth's speech to her troops at Tilbury in 1588 in which
she exhorted them to defend against the Spanish Armada

40 **element:** favourable environment

Ninepins.

THE KNAVE
Come to the point, Sir Walter.   25

WALTER
My point, then, Knave: there be no reason, if sweet reason doth permit, in enlightenment's bower—and reason says thou art the worthier man—

DONALD
Yes, Sir Walter, pray, merrily state the fulcrum of thine argument.

THE KNAVE
My colleague, although unframed and unreferenced, speaks 30 plain and true. That these toughs are those at fault, we are agreed; that I stand wounded, unrevenged, we likewise are agreed; yet you circle the meanings unconstantly, like blunted burrs, unstuck where they are thrown.

WALTER
I speak of aggression uncheck'd, as crowned heads of state once 35 spoke of Arabia—

DONALD
Arabia! Then we have put a girdle round the earth. On what does Sir Walter speak?

WALTER
Cast it from thy sieve-like books of memory, Sir Donald; thou art out of thy element.   40

DONALD
I know not of your 'element'; I should know more hereafter.

45 **doctor of physic:** physician. Walter is probably referring to
   Chaucer's learned character in 'The Physician's Tale,' one of the
   early episodes of *The Canterbury Tales*.

63 **man of middle earth:** a mortal existing on Earth, rather than
   on planes above or below

66 **speak plain:** i.e., make it clear

68 **rate of usance:** i.e., interest rate

The four classical elements.

WALTER
Wherefore was I curs'd only to minister
To congregations held in deafen'd pits?
I must hobble my speech; of elements, sir,
A doctor of physic did once explain   45
That all the earth is province elemental,
Sure and steady as the stone-wall foursome
A-holding up the Knave's roof, tied together
By power that we spake on, our traffic
Unmarred by thy rough and idle chatter.   50
And the complexion of the element
In favour's like the rug that ties the room.
O, a muse of fire the first element,
Airy breath the second; though this wind
May well be yours for all you flap your tongue,   55
O ill-dispersing wind of misery!
Thou hast no wings, and, liable to plunge,
You fit not fowl; yet foul your interruption,
Fish'd for facts, yet fish you cannot be;
So water, elemental third, you're not,   60
How much salt water thrown away in waste.
Of earth, no woman left on earth will have thee,
No man of middle earth will tend thy land,
So walk the plains like to a lonely dragon;
I care not.   65

THE KNAVE
Good sir, speak plain. I know not these villains; surely would
I ne'er traffic with this man of Orient birth who so abused my
rug. I have not the facility to present him with the rate of usance
and demand money in kind for that which he has spent upon't;
so I entreat thee, speak plain.   70

72 **man of Orient birth:** an émigré from Eastern Asia

72 **issue:** the matter in dispute

75 **line in the sand:** Walter is referring to a famous incident in military history. Gaius Popillius Laenas, Senator of Rome, confronted the invading Seleucid Emperor Antiochus IV Epiphanes and drew a circle in the sand around him as a warning. (Legend also has it that the outnumbered Spartan army drew a line in the sand at Thermopylae, although this is unverifiable.)

78 **nomenclature:** naming convention

79 **griefs:** grievances

84 **of high sentence:** of educated verbiage and lofty opinions. Walter here again quotes Chaucer, borrowing from his description of the Clerk.

89 **verily:** certainly, truly. Used frequently to fill a pause or render emphasis, as 'like' or 'man' in the modern vernacular.

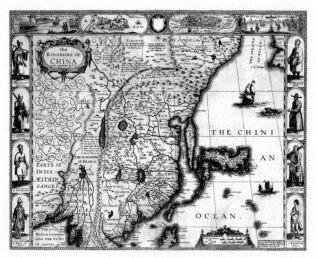

The Orient.

WALTER
I speak it well; my words are straight and true.
The man of Orient birth is not the issue.

DONALD
The Orient, Sir Walter?

WALTER
I speak, old friend, of truths in desert land.
The hour is nigh to draw line in the sand.   75

THE KNAVE
Deserts? I had made it plain that he was Orient-man.

WALTER
Though words in haste be only human nature,
'Orient-man' is not preferr'd nomenclature.

THE KNAVE
Give me no further counsel; my griefs cry softer than advertise-
ment.   80

WALTER
I speak of this other man, Sir Geoffrey of Lebowski. Is not thy
name, sir, Geoffrey of Lebowski? To be or not Lebowski, that is
the question; I see we still did meet each other's man. Shall we
not make amends? A gentleman of high sentence ought to be
of unsequestered location, possess'd of resources fit to restore a   85
thousand rugs from vile offence. He's not well married that lets
his wife a borrower be, such that men gravely offended bespoil
another man's rug. Be I wrong?

THE KNAVE
No, but verily—

94 **tide:** time. 'Miserable tide' also refers to the water passed on the Knave's rug, and hints at Shakespeare's love of sea accident as plot device: see *Twelfth Night* and *The Tempest*.

94 **rogues:** villains, vagabonds or otherwise disreputable sorts

94 **besmirch:** stain, sully

99 **ope:** open

103 **Marry:** a mild oath, derived from 'Mary' (i.e., the Virgin Mary)

'*Most miserable tide*'

WALTER
Be I wrong?   90

THE KNAVE
Yea, but verily—

WALTER
That rug, in faith, tied the room together, did it not?

THE KNAVE
By my heart, a goodly rug.

DONALD
And in most miserable tide did these rogues besmirch it.

WALTER
Prithee, Donald! Thou too eagerly hold'st the mirror up to na-   95
ture.

THE KNAVE
My mind races; I might endeavour to seek this gentleman Lebowski.

DONALD
His name is Lebowski? Verily, ope thine ear; that is thy name,
Knave!   100

THE KNAVE
On good authority; and his nobleness must oblige. His wife
taketh up quarrel and borrows, and they bespoil my rug.

WALTER
Marry, sir, my heartstrings do you tug;
They urinate upon thy damnèd rug.

Exeunt severally.

5 **twelvemonth:** year

7 **Queen:** probably not Elizabeth. The work is not set precisely in Shakespeare's own time, but mixes characters from several historical moments and mindsets. Assuming *Two Gentlemen* is set in England, the best candidate for the King in question is Edward III, who built up the military, revised the tax structure, reinforced the notion of English exceptionalism, and reigned into old age. He enjoyed great popularity in his own time, but was subject to more critical views thereafter.

SCENE 3

THE BIG LEBOWSKI's castle. Enter THE KNAVE and
BRANDT.

BRANDT
My lord is a man of accomplishment of many years, good travelling Knave; I pray you examine these honours and colours,
proof of life well lived. See here, the key to an old city, once
defended against man and beast; and there, a commendation
for men of business, bestow'd not by the twelvemonth but by   5
the mettle of the man.

THE KNAVE
Is that the Queen I see before me, render'd in oil-paints?

BRANDT
Indeed that is Sir Geoffrey of Lebowski, attending the Queen
in humble fealty, during her blessèd reign; as Queen, I remind
you, not as Princess.   10

THE KNAVE
Faith, an excellent tale.

BRANDT
I have not yet told all; indeed Sir Lebowski did counsel the King
himself, it is said, though, alas!, uncaptured in timely artistry.

THE KNAVE
A man of many faculties.

BRANDT
As many as capabilities, yet always one to boost his reach. Here   15
you may glimpse a record of his children.

19 **issue:** offspring

21 **loins:** euphemism for genitals

22 **cuckold:** a man whose wife, who *is* the issue here, is cheating on him. Cuckoldry is a favorite Shakespearean trope.

28 **smoking of the pipe:** not necessarily tobacco. Recent excavations of Shakespeare's Stratford home have revealed evidence of cannabis. Furthermore, in Sonnet LXXVI, he claims to 'keep invention in a noted weed.'

28–29 **armoury:** military storehouse for weapons and ammunition

31 **comedy of errors:** a lighthearted play, often featuring mistaken identity as a plotline—another favorite Shakespearean device

Cannabineae.

THE KNAVE
A care-crazed father of many children; it is a wise father that
knows his own child. An excellent list for a man of no doubt
excellent issue.

BRANDT
An amiable jest! Nay, I'd call'd his children his, but they come   20
not of his loins, thou understand'st.

THE KNAVE
A cuckold, he?

BRANDT
A most subtle jest! Nay, but children of the inner city, of good
promise, sworn to study but without the means. My lord re-
solves that they will all attend the university.   25

THE KNAVE
Verily!—Mine own years in the university hath fled my memory, though I recall some happy hours in the homes of various
headmasters, the smoking of the pipe, breaking into the armoury, and playing at ninepins.

            Enter LEBOWSKI, on a cart. Exit BRANDT.

LEBOWSKI
Marry, sir!—You be Lebowski, I be Lebowski, 'tis a wondrous   30
strange comedy of errors. But I am a man of business, as I imagine you are; tell me what you'd have me do for you.

THE KNAVE
Sir, I possess a rug, that, i'faith, tied the room together—

LEBOWSKI
You sent Brandt a messenger on horseback; he inform'd me.
How dost thou find me most fit for business?   35

43 **shower of gold:** a possible reference to the Titian painting *Danaë and the Shower of Gold*. The 1554 oil-on-canvas piece depicts Zeus descending to Earth to impregnate a woman; this wording might foreshadow the Knave's tryst with Maude. In his biography *Lives of the Artists*, Giorgio Vasari notes that Michelangelo critiqued the painting harshly, citing Titian's inattention to technique as proof that artists from Venice were lazy.

THE KNAVE
They sought thee, these two gentlemen—

LEBOWSKI
I shall repeat; you sent Brandt a messenger on horseback; he
inform'd me.

THE KNAVE
Then thou art aware 'twas thy rug, sir, that was the target of
this crime.   40

LEBOWSKI
Was it I, sir, who had a varlet's gift
To rain a shower on commanded rugs,
And set it in a shower of gold, i'faith?

THE KNAVE
Not in person, sir—but if a man is his name, and his reputation
his indelible inkstain, surely thy sea of care is tormented; what   45
tongue shall smooth thy name?

LEBOWSKI
Make me to understand, sir, for you are slow of speech as I of
step, and I am unsatisfied in motive. When upon any carpet
consideration the rain it raineth within these city walls, must
I stand accountable? Or are you as one of a thousand rogues,   50
fishing for sixpence betwixt another man's purse-strings? Are
you a labourer, Master Lebowski, earning that you eat, getting
that you wear?

THE KNAVE
Let me not to the marriage of false impressions deny impedi-
ments. I am not Master Lebowski; thou art Master Lebowski. I   55
am the Knave, call'd the Knave. Or His Knaveness, or mayhap

59 **abide:** subscribe to a highly respectable philosophy
60 **sirrah:** a condescending form of address to a man considered to be in lower social standing than the speaker
60–61 **pledge fealty:** swear allegiance
62 **motley:** a garment of many colours, the traditional costume of jesters and fools; wearing motley showed they were excluded from sumptuary laws (laws that reinforced existing social hierarchies by restricting the purchase of clothing, food, and luxuries) and marked their (lack of) place in the social order. The fool was of no class; he was simply a man for his time and place.
62 **jack-a-dandy:** a foppish, impertinent person
71 **shrewish:** difficult and unpleasant

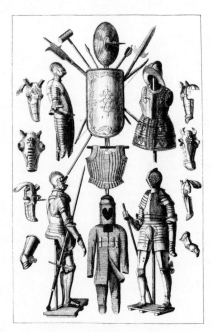

Armour.

Knaver, or mayhap El Knaverino, in the manner of the Span-
iard, if brevity be not in thy soul nor wit. A Knave by any other
name would abide just as well.

LEBOWSKI
Hast thou employment, sirrah? Surely you hope not to pledge   60
fealty nor till the earth in such roughly fashion'd armour, in-
vested in thy motley, clad as a jack-a-dandy on a Sunday?

THE KNAVE
I know not; what week-day, friend, is this?

LEBOWSKI
I tire, and cannot tarry; I am more busy than the labouring spi-
der, and dwell on the iron tread as a man of constant pursuits.   65
Thus, I pray you, you this way and I that way.

THE KNAVE
I must protest; the Knave mindeth. This will not stand, this
uncheck'd aggression; for your strength of mighty kings and
masters of the earth did not keep your wife from owing, a borrower and a lender being.   70

LEBOWSKI
How does my wife? She's not the issue here; my shrewish wife
hath a way with will, but I toil in hopes that she will shed her
frivolities, rash and unadvised, and live within her allowance,
which is in very ample virtue. Her mortal failures are her burden, as surely as your rug is your burden, and, verily, the bur-   75
dens of every man be his own, and 'tis in themselves that they be
thus or thus. I'll blame none for the loss of my legs. Some man
of Orient birth robbed them from me as spoils of war; faith,
who stole my legs stole trash, and I sallied forth and achieved in

80 **achievers:** those who have attained their goals by their own efforts; also, members of a valued fan base

82 **pox:** a curse or disease, often sexually transmittable

84 **condole:** mourn over, sympathise with

89 **gentle:** well-born, courteous

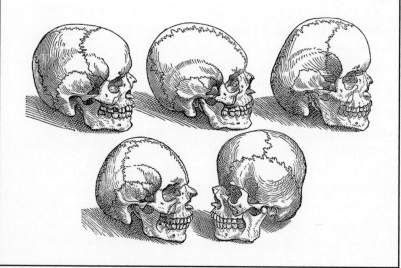

any aspect. Some are born achievers, some achieve greatly, and   80
some have achievement thrust upon 'em. Beseech me not!

THE KNAVE
Ah, a pox upon't!

LEBOWSKI
Indeed! 'A pox upon't!' 'Tis thine answer to everything. Your
merry revels have ended, sir. Let us condole the knight. The
rogues lost; the rogues have always lost, will always lose, and so   85
will it be tomorrow and tomorrow and tomorrow.

             Exit LEBOWSKI; enter BRANDT.

BRANDT
Good Master Lebowski. Did you enjoy meeting my honourable
lord?

THE KNAVE
Truly, sir, a nobleman most gentle;
He bade me take any rug in the castle.   90

             Exeunt.

SCENE 4

*Outside LEBOWSKI's castle. Enter THE KNAVE (with a
Persian rug) and BRANDT.*

BRANDT
I pray you, Knave, remember us in future visitations.

THE KNAVE
Faith, surely when next I near this neighbourhood, I will call
upon his lordship's good honour, and beseech his refreshment.

4 **verdant:** green, from the Middle French *verdoyant*

5 **hey-nonny-no . . . hey-nonny-nonny:** nonsense refrain for light-hearted songs (compare with 'na-na-na' today)

8 **blow:** as in modern slang usage

9 **good interest:** sexual reference, probably. As author Terry Pratchett puts it, 'the Elizabethans had so many words for the female genitals that it is quite hard to speak a sentence of modern English without inadvertently mentioning at least three of them.'

10 **common hump, where grass doth grow:** the mound on which a woman's pubic hair grows

11 **country:** a vulgar pun on a slang term for female genitals

11–14 **foot . . . south . . . maw . . . case:** double entendres

15 **serve your turn . . . cool my hot temper:** perform the sexual act

16 **painted lady:** prostitute

18 **tongue most moved:** i.e., capable of dexterous speech and cunning linguistics

Enter BONNIE and OLIVER.

BONNIE

[sings]

'With toe-nails of verdant and forester's green
With a hey-nonny-no and a hey-nonny-nonny   5
Blow thrice on my toe-nails and I'll be thy queen
And ever preserve me as thine, blithe and Bonnie.'

[to THE KNAVE]

I pray you, sir, blow.

THE KNAVE
Marry! But here's a lady of good interest, whose toe-nails are
the very green of the common hump, where grass doth grow   10
and where country lovers do foot. Whither shall I blow, maid?
For I am but a travelling tumble-weed, and may well be carried
by any wind, e'en south.

BONNIE
I mean only the wind in thine own maw in this case; blow, then,
serve your turn and cool my hot temper.   15

THE KNAVE
Sayest thou that I must blow upon thy foot, painted lady?

BONNIE
I ask this deed of you thrice now; and that which a damsel craves
constantly is the service of a tongue most moved in capability.
Look to my foot; I cannot reach that far. Blow, wind!

THE KNAVE
I fear thy charms. Will not thy consort mind   20
If I bestow his lady fair my wind?

23 **nihilist:** an adherent to a philosophical doctrine that denies that human existence has any intrinsic purpose, meaning, or value; from the Latin *nihil*, meaning nothing. No record of the term survives from Shakespeare's day, but the notion itself arises with surprising frequency in his work.

29 **gentle cock:** a reference to 15th-century bawdy poem ('I have a gentil cok / Crowyt me day . . .'). The author is unknown but suspected to be a Suffolk monk.

29 **help him to success:** i.e., cause him to achieve sexual climax

30 **shillings:** coinage established in the Tudor era, valued at one-twentieth of a pound

33 **Neptune:** the Roman god of water and horses

34 **humour:** temperament, attitude; also, bodily fluid

36 **ere:** before

A cock.

BONNIE
Nay, there's naught for which Oliver carest;
He mindeth not, for he's a nihilist.

THE KNAVE
O exhausting condition!

BRANDT
Our court's noble guest must not tarry, Lady Lebowski.   25

THE KNAVE
Lady Lebowski? Then thou art Bonnie? A merry wife indeed!

BONNIE
And a lady of good housekeeping and agriculture besides,
minded to economy and all practicalities. Were thou to bring
a gentle cock to my bed-chamber, I might help him to success
for ten shillings.   30

THE KNAVE
Such a lady of talents I have scarcely seen.

BRANDT
Yes, a most forthright jest! Free of spirit and good generosity,
she is the nimble nymph of Neptune, and we mark her with
good humour.

BONNIE
Free of spirit but ne'er free for flesh. Were I to regale thee with   35
parts of my humour, I would not bid Brandt hear the play ere he
paid a shilling himself.

BRANDT
Hark, a marvelous jest; but, I pray you, we dare not tarry. Come,
Knave.

bowling green: a lawn used for bowls. Many towns had lawns and (more disreputably) alleys; private bowling greens were also a feature of upper-class gardens of the day. Lower-class greens and alleys might well have been sloped and uneven, and frequented by those unable to achieve on a level field of play.

2 **I had those words:** i.e., I heard that

2 **Jerusalem:** the holiest city in Judaism, now capital of the state of Israel

3 **An:** if

7 **Cynthia:** an uncommon name in Shakespeare's day; an alternate name for Diana, the Roman goddess of the hunt and of the moon. In addition to fueling the Knave's perception of Walter's own illogical, Dionysian tendencies, the divine name indicates Walter's 'worship' of his former wife.

9 **retrograde:** opposed

A bowling green.

THE KNAVE
Yea, I shall come, and then return with money,   40
Or lose the labour'd love of fair Bonnie.

Exeunt.

SCENE 5

*The bowling green. Enter THE KNAVE, WALTER (with a dog),
and JACK SMOKE, to play at ninepins.*

WALTER
Thy tale is the stuff of dreams, and yet a waking dream of will.
I had those words under a spreading tree in Jerusalem.

THE KNAVE
An I were dreaming afore, I care not, but do I dream anew?
What manner of beast bringest thou to our nightly sport?

WALTER
Marry, 'tis the remnant of a previous life's nightly sport. That   5
I was once a married man, thou knowest well; that the Lady
Cynthia was a great lover of dogs, thou know'st in lesser degree;
and the cur abandon'd has a tendency to dine upon chair-leg
and oaken table, most retrograde to my lady's desire.

THE KNAVE
Thou speakest in riddles.   10

WALTER
It hath been my charge to attend this cur ere my Lady Cynthia
return ashore from a voyage to the islands, commanded by Sir
Martin of Ackerman.

14 **cur:** dog

18 **lunatics:** insanity, from the Latin *luna*, moon—appropriate as Walter's crazed actions here stem from Cynthia

19 **horn:** referring to the horns or antlers worn by a cuckold

19 **shrew:** a sharp-tongued woman

21 **seek the isle within the brook:** engage in coitus

28 **husbandry:** the care and management of animals. Walter is punning on his former status as Cynthia's husband.

THE KNAVE
Thou bringest a cur to ninepins?

WALTER
I bring naught to ninepins. The dog is not attired by my hand to   15
play at sport, nor do I fetch it ale, nor shall he throw thy bowl-
turn in thy stead.

THE KNAVE
Why, this is lunatics! This is mad as a mad dog! Were I a cuckold of such horn, and an untamed shrew bade me mind her
animal passions on maiden voyages, whilst men of lesser virtue   20
did swim in foreign waters and seek the isle within the brook,
marry, I would cry out 'Go hang!' and leave the cur to fall where
he may. Can she not board the beast with some gentle farmer or
country shepherdess?

WALTER
I pray thee, speak not of rites of marriage; for here a man calleth   25
vinegar the wine he hath not himself imbibed.
The cur is one of consequence, admired
In circles of husbandry, with well-noted
Documentation of his qualities;
And if 'twere spook'd, it might lose hide and hair.   30
The cur hath parchments—

THE KNAVE
Hark, now bowls Jack Smoke.

WALTER
Thou cross'st the line!

JACK SMOKE
Your pardon, noble sir?

35 **cavalier:** a gallant gentleman or knight; or, used as an adjective, casual or carefree

40 **l'oeuf:** French for 'the egg,' i.e., zero; punning on 'love'

41 **frame:** box on a score-sheet, or perhaps a line in a book of gambling accounts. Betting ran rampant in the lower-class Elizabethan bowling alley and contributed to its spotted reputation.

43 **Smokey:** a pun on Smoke's name and insubstantial quality

45 **strain'd:** compelled, stirred by force

WALTER
Thou cross'st the line, Jack Smoke, O cavalier,   35
As clearly demarcated in our rules,
In tumbling past the throw. 'Tis play most foul.

JACK SMOKE
But see the pins struck down in fair play's course!
Knave, mark mine eight of nine pins; mark it eight.

WALTER
Not eight but l'oeuf; you'll mark it nought, O Knave,   40
And so we carry on to the next frame.

JACK SMOKE
Peace, Sir Walter!

WALTER
Smokey, this be not the foul jungles of the darkest East Orient.
This be ninepins. We are bound by laws.

THE KNAVE
Nay, Walter; the quality of mercy is hardly strain'd. But a frac-   45
tion of his toe tripp'd over the line, not God's line but man's. Of
late I have read much of toe-nails. Suit the punishment to the
action, and shame not Smoke in sport.

WALTER
O unrightful judge!
This forfeiture is set in iron law   50
As drawn by great authority of league.
One roll might well determine that our side
Advance to glory; or be instead retired
As moss upon a tree-stump, while the Smoke
Drifts out to wreaths and triumphs. Hear'st thou   55

61 **equivocate:** hedge, evade the truth

66–68 **world of pain . . . lake of fire:** hell; as a Jew, Walter may be thinking of Gehenna, which has a gate and a lake of molten fire. On the other hand, he may simply be paraphrasing *Troilus and Cressida*: 'With such a hell of pain and world of charge . . .'

71 **vulgar tongue:** common language

A world of pain.

The robin redbreast's call? If robin shall
Restore amends, we must serve justice
Here. Be I wrong?

JACK SMOKE
Yea, but—

WALTER
Be I wrong?   60

JACK SMOKE
Thy words are hard; I must equivocate.
Put up thy pen, that I may mark it eight.

WALTER
Nay! I do protest, and draw my sword;
It shall teach thee to disobey my word.
Mark none but none into that bowler's frame,   65
Else thou shalt enter into a world of pain.
A world of pain, think upon't; unhappy world!
A lake of fire, rich with damnèd souls,
Gulfs of anguish 'twixt vales of agonies.
Mark me; we stand at twisted, jealous gates   70
Of cast-iron, above which, in vulgar tongue, reads
'Here is a world of pain, thou enterest thus'.
My steel before thee, 'tis the last of keys
That might could lock these doors, and keep thee
From this world of pain, or with one flick   75
Ope its mashing maw, and summon winds
To cast thee down within; an excellent key!
Farewell to earthly delights, farewell to friends,
To fellowships and follies and amends.
The choice to spare thy passage through these trials   80

83 **put up thy sword:** put your sword back into its sheath. Possibly quoting Christ: 'Put up again thy sword into his place: for all they that take the sword shall perish with the sword' (Matthew 26:52).

85 **faculty:** cognitive or perceptual capacity; from the Latin *facultatem*, meaning power or ability

86 **arithmetic:** i.e., logical capability

89 **fig:** a worthless trifle or a rude gesture

95 **I'll none:** i.e., I will not comply

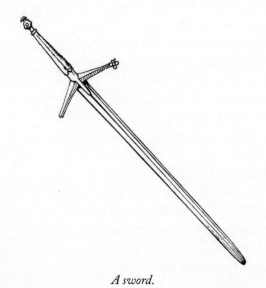

A sword.

Is thine alone; take heed, I entreat thee,
And turn thy back upon this world of pain!

THE KNAVE
Walter, put up thy sword; tarry a moment.

WALTER
Hath this whole world been mired in madness?
Remain ye men of faculty complete,   85
Of full arithmetic and prudence fair,
Attending to our noble bond and contract?
Or does here stand the last remaining man
To give a fig for rules and order yet,
No noble savage, but a stave unbroken   90
Who loves the law and bids it no misdeed.
I'll not be bent to lawlessness. Mark it nought, if we be men of
    honour.

THE KNAVE
Walter, the constable is notified. I pray you, sheath thy piece.

WALTER
Mark it nought, else I'll none.   95

JACK SMOKE
Good Sir Walter, speak with reason!

WALTER
Dost thou think I tarry idly? Mark it nought!

JACK SMOKE
Yea, I shall yield, and leave it to your pleasure.
Mark as thou wilt, in full and legal measure.

Exit JACK SMOKE. WALTER sits.

108 **pacifism:** an emotional problem

109 **beshrew me:** a mild oath

117 **Exeter:** the lowest bridging point of the River Exe. Its name
stems from the Celtic *isca*, or water, so this is probably a generic,
poetic reference to all water flowing under proverbial bridges.

119 **rakes:** debauchees; from 'rakehell,' itself from the Middle English
rakel, meaning hasty or headstrong

Pacifists.

THE KNAVE
In sooth, Walter, thou hast wounded me horribly.   100
Jack Smoke is cut of cloth alike my humour;
Peaceable men we, for peaceable times,
And Jack Smoke is a man of soft conscience.

WALTER
How absolute the Knave is!—
That he is conscious, I mark thee; I attend well.   105
In tender youth I dabbled in a course
To seek and hear moral philosophy.
Encount'ring pacifism on that road,
Though ne'er in Orient jungle, beshrew me; yet
I thought upon't e'en on fields of war.   110

THE KNAVE
Thou markest that Jack Smoke hath woes of mind.

WALTER
Faith, beyond pacifism?

THE KNAVE
He is a man of fragility, sir, and like to shatter.

WALTER
'Like'; yet I mark not his fragile dust,
Nor saw him break, nor melt, nor cleave in two.   115
The heated moment passeth, river-tide
Below a bridge in Exeter. Speak, Knave,
Are we not victorious in our sport?
We progress as do rakes; or be I wrong?

THE KNAVE
No, thou speakest true—   120

126 **fortnight:** two weeks

136 **Mesopotamian:** a resident of the region corresponding to parts of modern-day Iraq, Syria, Turkey, and Iran

An ass.

WALTER
Be I wrong?

THE KNAVE
No, sir, thy words are straight and true. But yet thou speakest
not, for thou hast not spoken but bray'd, in the manner of an ass.

WALTER
Fair; then I am an ass; let it be writ down that I am an ass. Then,
mark well: the Knave and his partner, an ass, shall play again at   125
ninepins in half a fortnight, their skills match'd against Joshua
Quince and Liam O'Brien. They worry me not; they shall be
o'er-push'd with certitude.

THE KNAVE
An we play again in seven days and seven nights, I pray you, be
of good humour.   130

WALTER
'Be of good humour!' 'Tis thine answer to everything.
Mark: thy peaceable nature, while conceived
In upright spirit, meant for noble deeds,
May cited be by devils for their purpose.
Mark well the Arab king in foreign land,   135
The base Mesopotamian, who lieth with steed.
Thou present'st to me a wall to hide behind
'Twas born of truce in fear and frighten'd mind.

THE KNAVE
I pray you, be of good humour.

WALTER
I am as calm as still waters, Knave.   140

143 **calmness:** placidity, serenity; a quality easily compared

152 **By carriage:** in addition to being a means of conveyance, 'carriage' refers to one's demeanour or behaviour. Brandt may be implying that Lebowski chose the Knave by his carriage, i.e., because of how he carries himself.

THE KNAVE
As steel waters, I'll warrant; put up thy
Icy blade! Crack not gory tales of war!

WALTER
My calmness exceeds thine.

THE KNAVE
Be of ease, I pray you! Be of good cheer,
And let us not repeat what happen'd here!   145

WALTER
My calmness exceeds thine. But hark; here comes a visitor.

Enter BRANDT.

BRANDT
All hail, good sir, honour'd Lebowski, hail!
'Tis I, one Brandt by name, humble servant still
To he whose name you recognise so well.
Wilt thou tarry with me a moment? Nay—   150
Fear not—we care not for the rug.
By carriage I would bring you to his lordship
Secluded in his castle's western wing,
Saith none to any man or good counsel,
Despondent to the last; thus I despair.   155
I call on thine assistance, gentle Knave.

THE KNAVE
Thou hast spoke plain, and I shall be thy guest.
Let us away to take Lebowski's quest.

Exeunt.

TWO GENTLEMEN
OF
LEBOWSKI

ACT 2

Flourish: ceremonial fanfare for a court scene

8 **Sans:** without, from the French

8 **loaden branches:** i.e., branches weighed down with heavy fruit or snow

12 **golden fire:** owning a home with fireplace and chimney indicated a higher economic class. Fire is also a traditionally masculine symbol.

ACT 2

SCENE 1

LEBOWSKI's castle. Flourish. Enter THE KNAVE, with
LEBOWSKI on his deathbed.

LEBOWSKI
Behold stark irony of hours dark.
As night betakes my heart, I cast mine eyes
Back across a lifetime of achievement,
Of challenge met, competitors surmounted,
Of roguish mankind's obstacles o'ercome,   5
Accomplish'd more than many dare to dream
In idle wishing; yet, remarkably,
Sans legs, like loaden branches, these my limbs
Imprison me from stature as a man.
But there's the thing, I ask; what is a man?   10
Be it reason, his faculty, his pose?
His act or expression, his golden fire?
What maketh well the piece of work of man?

THE KNAVE
Faith, perplexing questions, for a Knave.

LEBOWSKI
Mayhap the measure of a man is found   15

16 **pelf:** possessions

20 **Job:** the subject of a wager between God and Satan; possibly an additional crack at the Knave's lack of employment

26 **tests in cause betwixt his stance:** those organs that dangle between the legs

31 **suits of woe:** black clothes of mourning

36 **luminescence:** glowing light; as used here, a portmanteau of 'illumination' and 'essence'

Not in his store, his pelf, but in the storm
That tests him strong; the stabbing shocks of sin
That fix his courage to the post, and ask
If he be man, in times where men must stand
As Job was ask'd, or Jonah i' the fish,   20
Ne'er to sit silent, but to be of parts.
If man be man, he wears the mantle well,
Prepared to stand upright—forgive my text—
In tests that render price no virtue deem'd.

THE KNAVE
That maketh a man, in sooth; an a man were to lack those two   25
tests in cause betwixt his stance, 'twould be no man.

LEBOWSKI
You jest; but jesters do often prove prophets. My reeling
thoughts yearn for such simple counsel.

THE KNAVE
I aim to smoke of the pipe, if that betide your lordship's right
good health.   30

LEBOWSKI
Behold my trappings and my suits of woe;
Alas for Bonnie! So loving to her, I;
She is the light broke forth through yonder window,
From which my life is seen anew, the Sun
And Moon in equal measures, shining thus   35
On souls starved sick for want of luminescence.
And now do women's weapons, water-drops,
Stain my man's cheeks; a marvel fair—
But do you take surprise to mark my tears?

46 **rags and tatters:** in bits and pieces. Possible nod to same construction as 'lady of the Strachy' ('the lady of rags and tatters') as seen in *Twelfth Night*. This theory is best explained by Charles and Mary Cowden Clarke in *The Shakespeare Key* (London: Sampson Low, Marston, Searle & Rivington, 1879).

56 **pieces broke in eight:** the Knave confuses the Spanish dollar, worth eight *reales*, for the English pound. (The coin could literally be broken into eight pieces to make change.) Given the frosty state of affairs between England and Spain at this time, the Knave's conflation presumably reflects his negative view of Bonnie's captors.

THE KNAVE
Harking, nay. If moisture be the cost of love, weep on.   40

LEBOWSKI
O, it is excellent to have an achiever's strength, but, curious,
hath not a strong man a strong heart? Nay—strong men also
weep, the justice of the eyes severe, at once the infant, mewing
with a woeful ballad. Mark, a messenger did bring me dark
counsel ere noontime.   45

He gives THE KNAVE a note.

THE KNAVE
I mark thee; 'tis text of rags and tatters.

LEBOWSKI
It is a note of foul and odious tenor,
And hither have they sent it for her ransom.
Of cowardice and folly, not of men;
They who achieve not upon equal play   50
Nor even sign their names are scarcely men,
But weaklings, hideous beggars, sinners all!

THE KNAVE
Most curious and monstrous note this is,
Announcing they have captured Bonnie fair,
And for her safe return we'd send the rogues   55
A thousand pounds in pieces broke in eight.
'Instructions following; no punning jests'.
A foul, contemptuous deed! I mark thy pain.

LEBOWSKI
Of dark and cruel misdeeds I do know well.
Squire Brandt shall make you known of the details.   60

63 **courier:** messenger, from the Latin *currere,* to run
70 **murk:** darkness, from the Old Norse *myrkr*
71 **visages:** faces, countenances
74 **sexton:** not a sexual reference, for once

A courier.

Enter BRANDT.

BRANDT
My lordship's malady—unhappy hour!—
Forbids his action on this vilest act.
He seeks thy services as courier
To grant these thieves their ducats for their spoils
According to their wishes; thou would be   65
Offer'd a share in generosity.

THE KNAVE
Faith, a tempting offer; but wherefore doth his lordship seek my
qualities?

BRANDT
He hath recall'd thy sorry episode
Of rugs besoil'd, and villains in the murk.   70
An viewing varlet visages might aid
In rendering them punishèd, he sayest
'Twere best to have that knows the face of sin
And stands to tell the sexton that he sees.

THE KNAVE
Thou sayest his merry wife stands prisoner   75
Of those who were relieved upon my rug?

BRANDT
What may be true, I say not yes or no
Ere truth be found; in truth, we do not know.

Exeunt severally.

1 **strike:** a well-placed hit, attack
1 **palpable:** detectable, noticeable
6 **manhood:** one's Johnson
6 **page-boy:** a male servant, usually younger than fourteen years old
11 **paederast:** a participant in sexual conduct with an adolescent boy, from the Greek *paiderastia*

A paederast.

SCENE 2

The bowling green. Enter THE KNAVE, WALTER, and
DONALD, to play at ninepins.

THE KNAVE
A strike, a very palpable strike! O, but Quince can roll straight
and true.

WALTER
That he rolleth true, I cannot deny't, but the man rolls not
straight, for he is not a man to stand upright. To follow him
perverts the present path. Two seasons has he idled in prison for   5
exposing his manhood to a page-boy.

THE KNAVE
My lands!

WALTER
When first he came upon the holy wood, he was made to stand
in public gallows, and in such great letters as they write 'Here is
good horse to hire', it was signified on his sign, 'Here you may   10
see a paederast'.

DONALD
What manner of man be a paederast, Sir Walter?

WALTER
Hold thy tongue, Sir Donald.—Knave, what measure of moneys were thou offer'd?

THE KNAVE
Twenty pounds for mine own, and the matter of the rug for-   15
given. They may summon me at any hour day or night.

17 **in time of ninepins:** during the sacred hours set aside for a league
   match
27 **rug-pissers:** urinators upon a carpet or other domestic floor
   covering
35 **Muscovy:** the Russian province centred near Moscow

WALTER
An they should call for thee in time of ninepins, that would
hang us.

DONALD
What is like to happen in time of ninepins, Sir Walter?

WALTER
Peace, miserable villain; life will neither stop nor start at thy   20
command.

THE KNAVE
My purse is as good as filled; here is money found with ease.
I submit that the subtle lady may well indeed be her own ad-
versary.

DONALD
I'd know thy mind further, Knave.   25

THE KNAVE
This be not the traffic of harden'd thieves,
Nor rug-pissers, nor ruffians o' the night.
Look well upon a lady fair, so happy fair,
Who spurn'd her love for money, glitt'ring gold,
Where, much deprived of ample gifts and treats   30
Did scheme to steal a greater sum from some.
In owing much to much of men about
She sought devices to discharge her debt.

WALTER
O contemptible shrew!

THE KNAVE
As sure as what was said in Muscovy;   35

39 **walrus:** a tusked sea-mammal, also called a 'morse'; from the Old Norse *hrossvalr,* horse-whale. A surprising amount of information on Elizabethan walrus science is available in Emma Phipson's *The Animal-Lore of Shakespeare's Time* (London: Kegan Paul, Trench, & Co., 1883).

42 **hobby-horse:** a loose woman, easy to ride

43 **rank:** foul-smelling

43 **flax-wench:** a low-quality prostitute. Spinning or working with flax fiber was considered a lower-class occupation.

45 **Lenten:** i.e., given up for Lent (Walter is suggesting that Donald has taken leave of his senses); also 'lenten,' meaning short or lean.

48 **strumpet:** a prostitute. Possible etymologies for the term include the Latin *stuprare,* to have illicit sexual relations with, or *strupum,* dishonour or violation; the Middle Dutch *strompe,* stocking; the French *tromper,* to cheat or deceive; the Swiss *Strubel,* rude or unpolished person; the Low Saxon *strüne,* prostitute; and the list goes on. See Anatoly Liberman, *An Analytic Dictionary of English Etymology: An Introduction* (Minneapolis: University of Minnesota Press, 2008).

51 **fens:** swamps

A walrus.

'Look well to he whose benefit abounds
And knowest all', as I have tried to say.

DONALD
I am flabbergasted, overbowl'd,
As clumsy and unsettled as a walrus.

WALTER
O pernicious shrew!   40
His wife, Sir Knave! Go get you from the door.
His wife's a hobby-horse, deserves a name
As rank as any flax-wench.

DONALD
I be the walrus.

WALTER
Hold thy tongue, Donald! Thy mind is Lenten.   45
The quality of wealth has sicken'd me.
And had I known that this would come to pass
(O vilest strumpet! Sinner! Painted whore!)
I might have tarried ere accepting service.
War in far-flung jungles, as my friends   50
Did die face-down in mire and muck and fens!

THE KNAVE
I see connection not in argument
'Twixt Bonnie and the wars of Orient.

WALTER
'Tis not connected literally, as rope,
But yet by stardust, thought-string, tears, and hope.   55

58 **Hail, masters!:** Quince's interruption is best read in context. Bowling ascended to its rightfully great place in Elizabethan history in 1588, when, according to legend, Francis Drake was interrupted mid-game to be informed of the Spanish Armada's arrival near Cornwall. Quince's flamboyance should thus be read with a sneering Iberian overtone; given their victory, an English audience would have understood his confidence as just his opinion, man.

59 **Sodomites:** in Shakespeare's time, sodomy referred both to anal intercourse and other unacceptable behaviours, including child molestation and bestiality, considered acts of treason and capital offences. Sodomy was prohibited by a law in 1562 that strengthened an earlier 1533 statute against 'buggery.'

62 **By Jove!:** a mild oath, from the common name for Jupiter. It may allude to the tale of Jove and Ganymede, in which the god falls in love with a beautiful young man and makes him his page-boy.

68 **jade's tricks:** uncooperative and deliberately dilatory behaviour, like that of a 'jade' (an old and broken horse) refusing to move

70 **gizzard:** the ventriculus or gastric mill; also guts or innards

71 **Coriolanus:** Gaius Marcus Coriolanus, assassinated for his failure to betray Rome, as told in Shakespeare's *Coriolanus*

72 **Zounds!:** a mild oath, for 'God's wounds'

'Points up'

THE KNAVE
Look well, my friend; there be no connection.
Take to thy roll, thy play for our selection.

   Enter JOSHUA QUINCE and LIAM O'BRIEN.

QUINCE
Hail, masters! I crave thine able readiness
To be dealt with roughly, as the Sodomites.
For men of sport have noted that our play   60
In semifinal hour draws on apace.
By Jove! I'll wager well, Liam and me,
To thrash thee soundly at the fair tourney.

THE KNAVE
Yea, well, that be, forsooth, thy opinion, sir.

QUINCE
Well; but be forewarn'd. It reach'd mine ear   65
That combustible Walter, o'ercome with rage,
Did shed good sense, and raise his sword in play.
I fear not such jade's tricks, and seeing ill,
Would snatch the burden from the jealous knight
And pierce his gizzard with the wrongful steel,   70
Points up, as said of Coriolanus.

THE KNAVE
Zounds!

QUINCE
Thou speakest rightly, sir. No man misdeals with Joshua Quince,
by Jesu.

     Exeunt QUINCE and O'BRIEN.

81 **porter:** gatekeeper, from the Latin *porta*, gate

89 **short-hair'd damsel:** given the Elizabethan preference for long hair on women, this is possibly a nod to the practice of employing boys to play female characters on stage in Shakespeare's day

89–90 **flying carpet / From Arabian legend:** *One Thousand and One Nights* had not yet been published in English in Shakespeare's time. The stories, however, had been circulating for centuries, and some would have doubtless made it to a bustling city like London.

'The fireworks do city lanterns make'

WALTER
Nay, fear him not, nor his unworthy joys. 75
Recall the tragic tale of the page-boys.

Exeunt WALTER and DONALD.

THE KNAVE
Here I stand in sole on shrouded stage
To contemplate the bowls; a fitting sport
For men who serve to stand and then to fall.
But soft; what noise is this? Hark! Who's there? 80
Speak, if thou wouldst enter; I am no porter.

*Enter MAUDE and her VARLETS, unidentified. They strike
him, and exeunt.*

Again I bleed; wherefore do I attract
The wrongful slings and arrows of the land?
Who was't, mystery woman, craved my blood?
Who was't struck my jaw for satisfaction? 85
The fireworks do city lanterns make
And so I soar, down staring with a smile
Upon the place beneath; and seen ahead,
A short-hair'd damsel rides a flying carpet
From Arabian legend; here falls the Knave. 90
In sooth, I'm weary. Let us have a song.
'Tis well; for I have song for such a spell,
Reminded to me by befever'd dreams
Of man, and all that maketh mannish mettle
And what fair woman's task be in the battle. 95

[sings]

98 **sooth:** truth
99 **Fain:** gladly, happily

---

2 **emissary:** representative

A bridge.

'Behold a man to undertake quests brave
With little recompense for which to crave.
In sooth, Jove send a woman such as thee
Fain would discover true the man in me.'

Exit.

SCENE 3

A bridge. Enter THE KNAVE and BRANDT (with a sack of money).

BRANDT
The eightieth minute passes since their call,
Dispatch'd by emissary rough of speech.
So Knave, I charge thee, heed their every word,
Obeying all requests that they beseech.
Thy charge is simple: wait here all alone,　　　　　　　　　5
Let no man be companion to your end.
They spoke with crystal clarity; I dare
Not tarry long, lest they think me your friend.
What fate befell thy jaw, m'lord?

THE KNAVE
No mind.　　　　　　　　　　　　　　　　　　　　　　10

BRANDT
Then take these golden coins to leave behind.
Be wise and well, and heed the villains' plans:
I tell thee that her life is in thy hands.

THE KNAVE
Sir, I attend.

17 **Take pains:** make strong efforts, strive to succeed
18 **troth:** truth, faith
19 **dissolution:** acts of decay or indulgence, lacking in restraint
20 **witching hours:** the time of maximum power for ghosts, demons, and other supernatural beings, usually at midnight or from midnight to 3 a.m.
23 **ringer:** a proxy or substitute deployed in a foolproof scheme
27 **dervish:** a performer of Sufi dances that induce religious ecstasy
29 **jerkins:** short, sleeveless, close-fitting jackets worn over doublets
30 **French hose:** tight breeches

A ringer.

BRANDT
My lord did beseech me repeat that; hark well that her life is   15
in thy hands. Her life is in thy hands, Knave; I will attend thy
signal. Take pains. Be perfect. Adieu.

Exit BRANDT.

THE KNAVE
By troth! A life in hands as rough as mine,
In hands design'd for dissolution harsh.
What doth a Knave awake at witching hours?   20
But soft. Look sharp. Here's a strangeness indeed.

Enter WALTER, with a satchel.

WALTER
Hail, good Knave! I see you stand to linger.
Take of me this, I bring you here a ringer.

THE KNAVE
What devilry, sir? By whose direction found'st thou out this
place?   25

WALTER
Hours at my store have I spent weighing the motives and sensa-
tions of this crime, whirling like the dervish of faraway civili-
ties, to catch how the case was clad. Here in this satchel I have
weighed out my mud-stain'd trousers, my dirty jerkins, foul
French hose, and assorted motleys.   30

THE KNAVE
By my life, I see not why thou hast thy soiled vestments.

35 **hawk:** a plasterer's receptacle for mixed concoctions; unlike the Knave's later mention of eagles, this is not a reference to a despised predatory bird. The Knave is asking Walter if he intends to pass one tool (the ringer) for another (the actual bag of money).

44 **unfold yourself:** i.e., reveal your identity

45–46 **evening star:** a celestial light used in navigation; probably Venus

WALTER
We will not wait upon mine answer; for the answer is weight. It
is for the fullness of our pleasure that this very selfsame double
look not empty, but in equal scale.

THE KNAVE
Is thy invention to call a hawk a handsaw?   35

WALTER
It came upon me to think, as if rising from a dream, wherefore
it was our lot to settle for a plague-struck twenty pounds.

THE KNAVE
Wherefore the 'we', the 'our' in this hour?

WALTER
We could well own the thousand pounds in thy grasp, with no
man the wiser. Be I wrong?   40

THE KNAVE
Yea, I'll hazard all I have by it. At my word, Walter, this be not
a jest.

WALTER
At thy word, Knave, 'tis. Thou sayest she spirits herself.

      Enter several NIHILISTS, below, concealed.

NIHILIST
Who's there? Stand and unfold yourself.

THE KNAVE
Speak! I come carefully upon the hour. Steer us by the evening   45
star.

60 **amateurs:** lovers, from the French, itself from the Latin *amator*.
The modern use of the term (meaning hobbyist or dabbler) dates
from the 18th century; here, Walter questions the nihilists' manli-
ness.

64 **bescreen'd:** concealed, hidden

NIHILIST
'Us'? Hold thy tongue, or tongues if be ye two;
Your charge was to come in person only you.

THE KNAVE
Nay, I am one man, of several persons.
For each man in his time plays many parts,   50
His acts being two voices. Speak, friend!

WALTER
Knave, knowest thou the way to examine?

THE KNAVE
Peace, Walter! Thy presence does me ill.
Her life is in our hands; they're like to kill.

WALTER
Naught is bespoil'd; thou art not acting in the manner accord-   55
ing to a Knave. This above all: to thine own self be true. Let
him speak again.

NIHILIST
Hello there!

WALTER
Seest thou? Naught is bespoil'd. These rank villains are but
amateurs.   60

NIHILIST
Be not rash, unadvised, or sudden.
Knave, we shall proceed this time of meeting,
But do not feign, O witnesses above.
Toss down thy coin, to me bescreen'd in night.

2 **the big Lebowski:** the superior or less modestly achieving Lebowski. Some scholars contend that this name also refers to a now-lost play of that era, appealing to a ravenous and devoted base of theatregoers who would quote the work incessantly, analyse its underlying philosophy, and celebrate it with feasts culminating in ale, Maypole-dancing, and ninepins. The critical debate rages on.

3 **scheme and subtle gore:** a cunning, insidious plot involving violence

6 **selfsame:** i.e., one and the same

Bowling.

WALTER
Pass me the ringer, Knave; we'll hand it down.   65

THE KNAVE
I love thee, Walter, but thou art a fool.

They throw down the ringer.

WALTER
Here is thy purse, varlets, thy cheated prize.
The money's ours. Quick, Knave, thy chariot;
We'll bowl in friendship ere the sun arise.
Look sharp! A pox upon't, Knave; let us play at ninepins.   70

Exeunt severally.

SCENE 4

*The bowling green. Enter THE KNAVE and WALTER, to play
at ninepins.*

THE KNAVE
What hast thou done, Walter? What will we tell
The big Lebowski, who loves his wife so well?
I trust thee not for scheme and subtle gore;
The first thing they do, they'll kill the woman poor!

WALTER
Poor woman! Poor wench! You prattle on, O Knave!   5
Her captor and her self are the selfsame.
As so thou spake; and so still I believe.
She's no abusèd victim, but a thief.

THE KNAVE
Thou heardst me wrong; I said in idle thought

13 **Retain thy state:** i.e., stay in your current position or condition, do not change course. As Walter has already acted, the Knave may mean 'restrain thy state.'

22 **match of open air:** a game of bowls played outside. The public green was considered a more reputable place to play than an alley, and this is, after all, a league game.

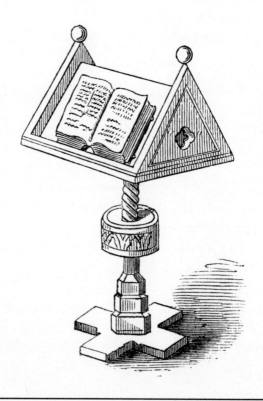

She might have selfsame stole; but whence the proof   10
And certitude thou hast to light this act?
What if thy certainty is all in vain?
Retain thy state and in consideration check
If majesty has fallen now to folly
In hideous rashness.   15

WALTER
I do assent
My certitude is one hundred per cent.

Enter DONALD.

DONALD
The jousts and games of sport continue on;
The looming tourney plans are posted high
And stand recorded in this schedule writ.   20

WALTER
Donald, hold thy tongue—no, stay, I err.
When do they set our match of open air?

DONALD
Faith, we face Joshua Quince and the Irishman this very Saturday.

WALTER
Saturday! Unhappy fortune. Something was forgotten in the 25
state of office. A calendar, a calendar! Look in the almanac; find
a date uncancell'd by destiny. What manner of fool is he that
scheduled this date? I did take pains to disclose my unavailability.

31 **slops:** loose lower garment, wide breeches
31 **low Dutch:** what we today simply call Dutch. 'High Dutch' would have referred to Germans.
36 **anon:** imminently
46 **Pomeranians:** a breed of small dog from Pomerania. The region is now eastern Germany, or part of Poland; this term subtly unites Walter's Polish Catholic ancestry and his dislike of Germans.

DONALD
Marry, 'twas Burkhalter.   30

WALTER
A German, all slops, or low Dutch; thrice I made him to know
that I roll not on Saturday.

DONALD
But posted it be; what's done cannot be undone.

WALTER
They shall unpost it, by my life!

THE KNAVE
I care not, Walter—what of that poor woman?   35

WALTER
Peace, Knave; she will tire of her little game anon, and wander
back in the manner of the punish'd cur, tail between her legs.

DONALD
Wherefore thou playest not at ninepins on Saturday, Sir Walter?

WALTER
On our most holy Sabbath I am sworn
To keep tradition, form, and ceremony.   40
The seventh and the last day rests the Jew;
I labour not, nor ride in chariot,
Nor handle gold, nor even play the cook,
And sure as Providence I do not roll.
Hath not a Jew rights? Hath not a Jew hands,   45
Organs, bowling-balls, Pomeranians?
If you schedule us, must you not do right?
If we step o'er the line, do we not mark it nought?
Holy Sabbath; I'll roll not, God-a-mercy.

50 **car:** chariot. Might be used colloquially here to mean a horse-cart or carriage. Shakespeare usually employed this term in reference to the sun god Phoebus, and the chariot that took the sun across the sky; this foreshadows the fiery fate of the Knave's vehicle.

51 **japes:** jokes, jests

56 **Alack the day!:** an expression of sorrow, mourning, or regret

59 **gull-crack'd:** deceived or taken advantage of, probably from 'gulled'

Amateurs.

THE KNAVE
I'll to my car; I must leave this place.   50
I tire of these arguments and japes.

DONALD
Stay, Knave; I'd hear of how ye handed off to criminals their
accursèd spoils.

THE KNAVE
There is naught to tell. All is lost. They did not get their money,
and they will kill—   55

WALTER
Yea, they will kill the woman poor. Alack the day! They will kill
the woman poor. Alas, poor woman! They'll kill her well.

DONALD
Walter, how dost thou proceed upon the Sabbath?

WALTER
Knave, I stand surprisèd, gall'd, gull-crack'd.
They will kill none, harm none, say none, do none.   60
Amateurs they, I'll take it to my grave,
And all Lebowski's money shall be thine. Be I wrong?

THE KNAVE
Walter, thou hast erred.

WALTER
Nay! For thou hast money in our car,
And they have taken linens mine afar!   65
My ragged hose bespoil'd, my dirty whites,
My breeches and my foulest-smelling tights!

81 **stridence sick:** harshness or vociferousness taken to cruel or unreasonable levels

82 **argosies:** merchant ships

A horse.

THE KNAVE
Hark! Look now to where my ride was park'd.
There it's not; the space is free and dark.

DONALD
Prithee, Walter, who hath thy breeches?   70

THE KNAVE
Ruin'd! Poor stolen car in a dead man's space.
My kingdom for a horse to catch these dogs!
The money, gone—mine only transport, gone—
They've robb'd me of that which enriches me
And left me poor indeed! Howl! Howl! Howl! Howl!   75
Call up the watch! O villainy, villainy!
O, I am fortune's fool, lost all, lost all!

      Exeunt WALTER and DONALD; enter MAUDE.

You there, close-cropped woman all in green.
Be you shapes and tricks or vile apparition,
Say, why is this? Wherefore? What should we do?   80
See you the shameful souls of stridence sick
Plunder'd my argosies most grievously?

MAUDE
By Maude Lebowski I am call'd in faith.
I came to you by night in this same place
To be revenged for your ill-gotten prize.   85
Your jaw was punch'd, your rug whiskèd in haste
Not hours after you had brought it home.
Why doth God make us love His goodly gifts
And snatch them straight away? We'll know it yet.

I'd have you be my guest in my abode,   90
My studio of arts, my academe.

THE KNAVE
Lo, the rug Lebowski gave to me?
Thou art the lady caused me injury.
So I'll with you to see about my carpet,
And hope for fairer wind about my chariot.   95

Exeunt.

TWO GENTLEMEN
OF
LEBOWSKI

ACT 3

ACT 3

SCENE 1

An artist's studio. Enter THE KNAVE and MAUDE.

MAUDE
If by my art, my curious friend, I have
Put the wild notions in a roar, so be't.
What think you on the female form, O Knave?
The woman's part in me so gallantly
Manifests itself within mine art   5
Commended by the wise as country work;
I paint only those of my own sex.
The very word is said to bother men,
Discomfort them, encircled in their ring.
It is the very painting of discomfort,   10
Two legs without a head. I say no thing.

THE KNAVE
I take no awkward pause, nor balk nor stare,
But only ask, askance, what art this is.
I see no ring to mar if I would kiss't,
But only oily painting I might stain.   15
The Knave deciphers nothing in its image;
Thy work has made a nihilist of me.

23 **King Richard the Third:** the last king of the House of Planta-
genet, and the central character of one of Shakespeare's histories;
also, one's selfsame Johnson

24 **rod:** a sexual pun on the unit of measurement—about five metres,
derived from the average length of a medieval ploughman's ox goad

26 **Benjamin Jonson:** playwright, poet, and urban achiever. A contemporary of Shakespeare's, his best-known works include *Volpone*
and *The Alchemist*. Although it is not clear how close he and Shakespeare actually were, Jonson's eulogy for the Bard is well-known:
'He was not of an age, but for all time,' and not exactly a light-
weight.

29 **marquess:** the female equivalent of a marquis; in British peerage,
the title below duke and above earl

Men with a rod.

MAUDE
In faith, the art is only what you will,
And if the word can poison not your ear
Then you're in luck; some men of lesser stuff   20
Dislike to hear it, dare not speak its name.
Whereas without a flicker of his eye
A man might speak of King Richard the Third,
Or pose an idle sonnet on his rod,
Or praise the wit of his selfsame Johnson.   25

THE KNAVE
As Benjamin Jonson, lady?

MAUDE
Let us speak plain and to the purpose. My father bade you take
the rug, but that you chose was, in faith, a gift from me to my
departed mother, the happiest gift that ever marquess gave, and
thus not his to make a rich and precious gift of. But trifles,   30
trifles; let us speak of this supposed kidnapping. It hath the
rankest compound of villainous smell that ever offended nostril.

THE KNAVE
Permit me to explain about the rug—

MAUDE
What cares have you, Lebowski, upon love?

THE KNAVE
Alack, lady, thy question does me vex.   35

MAUDE
The physicality of making love;
I'd have you tell me if you like it well.

38 **women of my stripe:** i.e., women of my type. 'Stripe' here could also mean the scar or bruise from a beating; Maude may be hinting at sadomasochism or harness play.

42 **satyrs:** male woodland creatures with goatlike qualities and insatiable appetites for sexually-charged revelry; from Greek mythology

43 **nymphs:** nubile special ladies, fond of coitus; literally, 'tree dwellers,' from Greek mythology

44 **Oberon:** the king of fairies—a real reactionary

55 **'Log Jamming':** a mass of logs crowding a river and creating an impasse. This portentous imagery suggests that perhaps the cable never will be fixed.

A woman (l.) with a satyr.

A myth persists on women of my stripe,
That our body politic renders us in hate
Of acts of love; a most injurious lie.   40
The enterprise can have in it much zest.
But men who walk with satyrs in the morn
And women swimming nightly 'twixt the nymphs
Are punishèd by Oberon for sin
And do the deed compulsively engaged,   45
Sans joy, sans love, sans everything.

THE KNAVE
Prithee nay!

MAUDE
So damn'd a soul is Bonnie; I have heard
That lustful creatures sitting at a play
Have by the cunning language of the scene   50
Been struck so to the soul that presently
They have proclaim'd their infatuations.
I've had these players make their show for you,
Suiting the action to the word indeed.
It shall be called 'Log Jamming', because   55
It hath bared bottom; but hark—the players.
So please your grace, the Prologue is address'd.

*Enter OLIVER as the PLAYER KARL HUNGUS, BONNIE
as the PLAYER WHORE, and a PLAYER QUEEN.*

PLAYER QUEEN
Two women, both alike in beauty,
In fair Verona where we lay our scene,
From broken cable break to new nudity,   60

64 **rid:** had sex with

65–66 **beast with two backs:** an unseemly sexual act. The phrase is most famously found in Shakespeare's *Othello*, but it is not an original coinage—a version was used by Rabelais in *La vie de Gargantua et de Pantagruel,* c. 1532. ('These two did oftentimes do the two-backed beast together, joyfully rubbing and frotting their bacon 'gainst one another.')

69 **The cable broke:** Karl Hungus is describing a nautical disaster, again in keeping with Shakespeare's interest in the theme. See *Henry VI, Part 3.*

73–74 **I should have old:** i.e., I would wear myself out

74 **turning his key:** sexual reference, exactly what it sounds like

Cable, unbroken.

Where civil breasts touch civil hands unclean.
The which if you Jaques Treehorn's play attend,
What this fine miss and whore shall strive to mend.

THE KNAVE
She hath rid her prologue like a rough colt.

MAUDE
Such riding you will see the like of, so as to form the beast with   65
two backs. But hark; here is the poor player that struts and frets
to play Karl Hungus upon the stage.

OLIVER
I rode to thee dispatched with all speed.
The cable broke, the holding-anchor lost.

THE KNAVE
Marry, I know that man; he is a nihilist.   70

MAUDE
And is her face familiar to you;
Familiar and by all means vulgar?

BONNIE
Knock, knock! Never at quiet. Here's a man of repair; I should
have old turning his key. Hark to my noble kinswoman, here to
travail in a shower brought up by a tempest of the soul.   75

PLAYER QUEEN
Hast thou, traveller, perform'd to mend the cable that she bade
thee?

MAUDE
This is the silliest stuff that ever I heard.

80 **fatuous:** foolish, silly

83 **parlance of our times:** the contemporary idiom or style of speech; from the French *parler*

90 **fornicator:** a wanton practitioner of coitus; from the Latin *fornix*, underground brothel

103 **thorough:** Maude's emphasis on the doctor's thoroughness may be Shakespeare's commentary on the bold if misguided state of medicine of the day. Further information available in *The Medical Mind of Shakespeare* by Audrey C. Kail (Balgowlah, New South Wales: Williams & Wilkins, 1986).

A man and woman, neither one fixing the cable.

THE KNAVE
I wonder if he be to fix the cable.

MAUDE
Be not fatuous, Geoffrey. It matters not   80
A fig to me if Bonnie be a whore,
Nor that she courts the merry Jaques Treehorn,
To use the happy parlance of our times.
But our good name Lebowski is such stuff
As dreams are made on for a host of youth   85
Whose education our foundation builds,
And proud we are indeed of all of them.
My father stole much money from these babes
To pay the thieves to purchase back his wife.
The fornicator, devilry-compulsed,   90
Hath took my father on her sinful ride.
As for thy rug, I charge thee with a task;
My father's crime too loathsome for the law,
His scandal being ruinous to our name,
I bid thee find the money that thou pass'd   95
These villains and return it to my keep;
I'll pay thee handsomely in fine reward
That thou canst purchase any rug thou wilt.

THE KNAVE
The task is right in purpose and in law,
But wherefore didst thou crack me on my jaw?   100

MAUDE
Pardons, good Geoffrey. I know of a learnèd doctor to examine
thee, with no physician's bill expressly charged. He is an honourable man, and thorough.

106 **borough:** a town granted self-governance by the Crown in medieval times. The term may stem from Alfred the Great's system of autonomous burghs; the concept survived the Norman conquest even though the burghs did not.

---

beverage: a flavoured drink, generally 'hard' or 'soft,' meaning alcoholic or non-alcoholic; from the Old French *boivre*, to drink

6 **shag-hair'd:** i.e., with rough and untamed hair

A maggot.

THE KNAVE
Thy thought is kind.

MAUDE
See the doctor, he's honourous and thorough;   105
After thou returnst to thy good borough.

              Exeunt severally.

SCENE 2

Upon the road. Enter THE KNAVE, with a beverage; opposing,
enter BRANDT and LEBOWSKI (on his cart).

LEBOWSKI
Speak, and speak quickly, foul vagrant!

THE KNAVE
I beseech ye, there be a beverage here.

BRANDT
Our attempts to reach thee have been frantic and numerous,
Knave.

LEBOWSKI
Whither my money? Thou were under thy master's command   5
transporting a sum of money. Thou liest, thou shag-hair'd villain! Thou odious maggot! Her life was in thy hands!

BRANDT
Verily, this be our concern, Knave.

THE KNAVE
Pray, naught is bespoil'd here—

10 **Zeus's noble chariot:** Zeus, the chief Greek god, commanded a chariot of gold. Unlike in Christianity, Greek gods would regularly join the mortal realm and partake in mortal practices like sex and gravity.

12 **'we' of royalty:** *pluralis maiestatis,* the use of a plural pronoun to refer to a single person of high status

25 **a wilderness of monkeys:** unknown

30 **equerry:** a senior attendant within a household; from the French *écuyer,* squire

30 **excises:** taxes

A monkey.

LEBOWSKI
Naught is bespoil'd? Zeus's noble chariot hath crashed into   10
yonder mount!

THE KNAVE
We, forsooth, the 'we' of royalty,
Did drop the money as instructed hence.
But certain things reveal'd to breaking light,
Occurring not to ye; of nature such   15
That blaming me will win ye not the lass.

LEBOWSKI
What dost thou prattle on, O blith'ring fool?

THE KNAVE
I speak of information borne anew!
I blither of the new stuff come to light!
Know ye she hook'd herself away? 'Tis true!   20
A lady happy fair, spurn'd, thou knowest,
In the parlance of our time, ne'er borrower
Nor lender be, to known nymphs and satyrs;
Yet I am well, I am well. She must feed
A wilderness of monkeys; occurr'st that?   25

LEBOWSKI
In faith, Master Lebowski, it occurr'd not.

BRANDT
It had not occurr'd to us, Knave.

THE KNAVE
That it occurr'st not to ye, I forgive, for ye be privy not to the
new stuff; that is why I am charged. As such, might we speak of
settling accounts? Mine equerry feareth for mine excises.   30

31 **least wholesome:** most evil

---

3 **Vexatious:** perplexing, worrisome

A tavern.

LEBOWSKI
Present to him the worst and least wholesome envelope, Squire
Brandt.

BRANDT gives the envelope to THE KNAVE; within, a toe.

O Knave! Since thou hast failed to achieve
The brief and modest task that was thy charge,
Stolen my pelf, and still betray'd my trust,   35
I've told these varlets thou hast took their prize,
Encouraged them to seize their bond from thee.
With good Squire Brandt as witness to my vow
I promise thee that any harm to Bonnie
Shall visit tenfold time upon thy head.   40
Ope thy parcel, sinner! See her toe,
Chopp'd off from her and still bepainted green.
Now it is said; 'tis all thou needs must know—
For I will not abide another toe.

Exeunt severally.

SCENE 3

A tavern near the bowling green. Enter THE KNAVE and
WALTER.

WALTER
My lord, I do deny it is her toe.

THE KNAVE
Whose toe be it, if not my lady's toe?

WALTER
Vexatious problem that, but not of heft.
There's naught to indicate the lady's harm'd.

8 **favour:** appearance
14 **cockerel:** rooster
15 **soil'd with fear:** i.e., so afraid as to soil ourselves

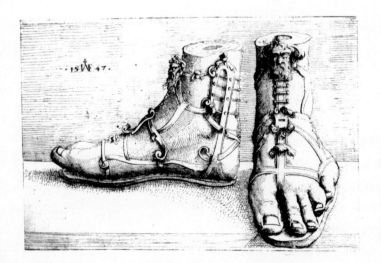

THE KNAVE
The fresh green paint of fairest Bonnie's nail!   5

WALTER
Marry, sir, nail-painting, rugs, and urine.
A man may paint the white toe green, tell her,
Paint an inch thick, to this favour she must come.

THE KNAVE
And where might a man fetch a toe?

WALTER
O toe!   10
Thou wouldst have a toe? A toe can be obtain'd.
Ways are known, Knave. Thou wilt not like to hear.
I'll have a toe for thee this afternoon
Ere singeth cockerel at three o'clock.
These amateurs would have us soil'd with fear.   15

THE KNAVE
They'll kill her, Walter, ere they turn on me.

WALTER
Thy stress is great, imper'ling thy reason;
This be a string of crimes with victims none.

THE KNAVE
But thou hast not explain'd the cursèd toe!

WALTER
I pray you, think no more upon the toe!   20

Enter MISTRESS QUICKLY.

21 **temperance:** the cardinal virtue of moderation
24 **prior restraint:** the outmoded legal practice of shackling a suspect before a crime has been committed; a corruption of basic freedoms
25 **smote:** struck down
30 **without:** outside, but also punning on the Knave having left 'without' drinking

MISTRESS QUICKLY
I remind ye, sirs, to acquire and beget a temperance that may
give thy voices smoothness, trippingly on the tongue. This tavern be a place of family business.

WALTER
Nay! The Courts consider'd prior restraint
And smote it thus; I'll speak my chosen piece.   25

MISTRESS QUICKLY
If patience cannot calm thy storm forthwith
Fain would I bid thee leave my tavern-door.

WALTER
My friends did die face-down in mire and muck
That you and I might trade within these walls.

THE KNAVE
Nay, I'll none; I take my leave without.   30

> *Exeunt all but WALTER, severally.*

WALTER
Knave, prithee stay! This doth affect our tale!
Our freedom's base! I'm finishing my ale.

> *Exit.*

SCENE 4

> *THE KNAVE's house. THE KNAVE is in his bath.*

THE KNAVE
I am conducted to a gentle bath.
Will all great Neptune's ocean wash this Knave
Clean from the land?

Alarums: call to battle or arms

marmot: a large ground squirrel that feeds on grasses, mosses and lichens; possibly amphibious

---

7 **lance:** euphemism for penis; see also most nouns in Shakespeare

A marmot.

Alarums. Enter OLIVER and the two NIHILISTS, bearing a marmot.

Forsooth! This be a place
Of residence, and much a private place.—   5
O excellent marmot!

OLIVER
Anon, we crave the money, Lebowski.
We speak in neither jest nor fallacy.
We could do such stuff as dreams do feature,
Believing in nothing; empty and void.   10
Tomorrow if thou hast the ransom not
We shall recourse, and off thy Johnson cut.

Exeunt severally.

SCENE 5

The tavern at the bowling green; enter THE KNAVE, WALTER, and DONALD, to sit at the bar.

THE KNAVE
My car is found, but treasure none within't,
Although the constable has sworn to find't.
My inquiries of leads led him to mirth
As if my misery and woes to scorn.
O piteous Knave!—My only hope remains   5
That in his anger, the Lebowski big
Kills me ere these Germans cut my lance.

WALTER
Ridiculous, good Knave. Thou knowest well

9 **eunuch:** a man castrated for social or religious reasons

11 **Doctor Faustuses:** as in *The Merry Wives of Windsor,* a reference to the title character of the popular play *The Tragical History of Doctor Faustus* by Christopher Marlowe. A contemporary of Shakespeare's, Marlowe's work also influenced the Bard's *The Merchant of Venice* and inspired a host of controversial authorship theories.

12 **usurpers:** illegitimate claimants to power or a title, often taking it by force or subterfuge

14 **geld the lily:** to cut off a man's testicles, or more colloquially, to deprive one of an essential part

That no man makes thee eunuch while I live.
Naught hath changed; these German swine are cruel, 10
Three German devils, three Doctor Faustuses,
Mere usurpers, tyrants, and what's worse.

DONALD
Were't they tyrants, Knave?

WALTER
They meant to geld the lily, Sir Donald!
Split never hairs tonight. Or be I wrong? 15

THE KNAVE
Nay; not tyrants. Nihilists to a man.
They believe in nothing; nothing will come of't.

WALTER
Nihilists! I am beshrewn. Say what thou wilt
Of tyrant's tenets, Knave; it seeks to stand
Philosophy and politic, not void. 20
And let it noted be that wildlife kept,
Amphibious rodent, in domestic walls,
Is retrograde to right and civil laws.

THE KNAVE
Art thou a forester? A woodcutter yet, or shepherd of the flock?
Who cares a fig for th'accursed marmot? 25

WALTER
I speak only to sympathise, Knave.

THE KNAVE
I need no sympathy or pitied whine.
That which I need is only Johnson mine!

30 **Wouldst thou . . . ?:** i.e., Do you wish to?

30 **sad:** sober, melancholy

44 **sarsaparilla:** a trailing vine native to Central America used medicinally and to flavour beverages

45 **Indian:** or possibly 'Judean'; see *Othello*. In this case the word is probably 'Indian,' if only because Judas Iscariot's views on sarsaparilla remain unknown.

DONALD
Wherefore needest thou that, O Knave?

WALTER
Be of good cheer, friend. Wouldst thou enter the tourney so sad?   30

THE KNAVE
A pox upon the tourney! And thee, Walter!
I might have escaped this with few pains
But for the shock of stench upon my rug.
Now I am cursed with damages tenfold
In seeking counsel from so great an ass.   35

WALTER
'A pox upon the tourney', he declares.
Come, then, Donald; we'll leave him as he fares.

Exeunt WALTER and DONALD.

THE KNAVE
O, that these two, two solid friends would leave
Me to resolve myself on what to do.
Two noble kinsmen, nay?—Another ale.   40
Why, then, the Russian White my only drink;
Let's drink together friendly and embrace.

Enter the CHORUS.

CHORUS
What sayst thou, Mistress Quickly? Hast thou a goodly beverage, brew'd of sarsaparilla-root?

MISTRESS QUICKLY

[without]

As brew'd in the city of the base Indian.   45

50 **bear:** a stocky mammal reputed to consume and be consumed by humans. The sport of bear-baiting, where dogs would be set on restrained bears for public amusement, was wildly popular in the Elizabethan era, with Queen Elizabeth herself so favouring the pastime that in 1591 she outlawed play performances on Thursdays so they would not conflict with the weekly bear-themed entertainment. Here, the word might also be 'bar,' an obstacle or impediment.

53 **fashion:** personal style

56: **crave a boon:** ask for a favour

A bear.

CHORUS
Ay, there's a good one. How fares the Knave?

THE KNAVE
So foul and fair a day I have not seen.

CHORUS
Such a day, I mark thee, whereupon the winter of our discontent
is ne'er made glorious summer. A gentleman wiser than myself
did say that on some such days, thou exits, pursued by a bear,   50
and on others, the bear exits, pursued by you.

THE KNAVE
By my troth, a good philosophy. Was't of the Orient?

CHORUS
Nay, far from it. I mark well thy fashion, good Knave.

THE KNAVE
And I thy fashion, stranger.

CHORUS
Many thanks.   55
If I may crave a boon, may I request
That thine ungracious mouth be less profane,
Spoke less in cursing word, and more in craft?

THE KNAVE
What dost thou speak upon, O damned fool?

CHORUS
I jest; well-spoken, Knave. Be of good ease;   60
Exeunt now, the tumbling tumble-weeds.

Exeunt.

Knox Harrington: Maude suggests that this artist is so well-known that the Knave should recognise him by name. If the character does have a basis in history, he might be Sir John Harington, godson of Queen Elizabeth, who was well known to her court for his wit and epigrams—as well as for inventing a forerunner to the flush toilet. (Given the Knave's urine-based misadventures in Act 1, this could explain his instant dislike of Knox.) Harington's jests went a little too far, and his popularity was in decline as Shakespeare's star ascended; perhaps this character's name is a stab at "noxious Harington.'

1 **pilgrim:** a traveller on a religious journey

3 **humour:** mood; punning on Harrington's laughter at a private amusement

11 **waylaid:** unavoidably detained

14 **hired player:** an actor retained on a freelance basis, not part of an established company

SCENE 6

MAUDE's studio. Enter THE KNAVE and MAUDE, with
KNOX HARRINGTON.

THE KNAVE
What manner of man is this pilgrim strange,
Who sits upon my lady's couch and laughs
As if in private humour of his own.
What is thy trade; what secret craft is thine?

KNOX HARRINGTON
You know. 'Tis nothing much to look upon,   5
Matters of no import. A bit of this;
A little bit of that; O, how I laugh!

MAUDE
Geoffrey, thou hast not seen doctor skill'd
Whose studio I ask'd thee to attend.
Hast thou heard news of money yet recouped?   10

THE KNAVE
In sooth, I must confess I was waylaid
And fear I must resign the charge at hand;
Oliver hath persuaded me to rest.

MAUDE
He is a hired player and a fool,
An actor poor, unexcellent musician,   15
Who'd play abductor for this fiendish plot.
Thou knowest well this woman is in health,
No more a victim than she mother'd me.

21 **titter:** giggle in a nervous or affected fashion
22 **parlay:** exploit or make investment of. The Knave means 'parley,' chat or converse.
Doctor Butts: possibly William Butts, the King's personal physician, also seen in Shakespeare's *Henry VIII*
29 **slide:** remove

A doctor.

THE KNAVE
This case perplexes me in complex course,
With many ins and many outs and strands.   20

KNOX HARRINGTON
Most mirthful! I'll titter thus upon't.

THE KNAVE
Beshrew me, who is this gentleman, Maude, to parlay in thy
parlour?

MAUDE
Knox Harrington, the tapestry artist. Geoffrey, thou hast not
seen the doctor, and I fear for thy bruise.—Enter, doctor!   25

Enter DOCTOR BUTTS.

I would not be to blame for pains delay'd.
And yea, he is an honourable man, and thorough.
Examine him, good doctor, as thou wilt.

DOCTOR BUTTS
Do slide thy breeches, Master Lebowski.

THE KNAVE
'Pon my life, I was stricken on the jaw.   30

DOCTOR BUTTS
'Tis well; but still thy breeches must be slid.

MAUDE
Come, Geoffrey. While the good doctor examines,
I'd have a song, if it pleases thee.

36 **monarch of the vine:** Bacchus, the Roman god of wine, grapes and fertility. This is a drinking song for a festive occasion.

39 **back-door mine:** this reference to a back-door (and adjoining yard, presumably) may indicate that despite being a deadbeat, the Knave was a man of lands

'Hey-nonny-no, looking from back-door mine'

THE KNAVE

[sings]

'Prove true, imagination,
To make a man sing blessings,   35
Hey-nonny-no, thou monarch of the vine;
Burthen me on the morrow,
Parting is such sweet sorrow,
Hey-nonny-no, looking from back-door mine.'

Exeunt severally.

TWO GENTLEMEN
OF
LEBOWSKI

ACT 4

9 **churl:** a rude, boorish person, from the Old English *ceorl*, peasant

10 **not born under a rhyming planet:** i.e., not a talented poet

12 **King of France:** unknown. Research on the King's identity and real estate holdings continues at the Université d'Orléans with the support of young scholars worldwide.

ACT 4

SCENE 1

A playhouse. Enter THE KNAVE, WALTER, and DONALD,
to hear the PLAYERS.

WALTER
Come, Knave; I'd hear the balance of thy tale.
Inside thy car didst thou detect some trace
By villains left, who deprived it of goods?
No ghost of guilt, identity betray'd
By careless thieves who cover'd not their tracks?   5

THE KNAVE
I found a document, so roughly writ
It troubled me to make good sense of it.
Of school-days' friendship, childhood innocence,
A paper writ in study by some churl
Of youth not born under a rhyming planet.   10
'Twas lesser verse composed and badly hewn,
Concern'd the King of France, and purchased land,
And though I am a weakish speller, I
Detected errors mark'd throughout in hand
Of school-master despair'd, in ink so red   15
At first the Knave had thought that he had bled.

20 **Laurence:** perhaps from St. Lawrence of Rome, a patron saint of students. He was martyred for stealing valuable Church treasure to distribute to the poor and then stonewalling the Prefect when questioned.

29 **Bulk:** majority; from the Old Norse *bulki*, a ship's cargo

30 **dunce:** a fool or simpleton, incapable of learning; the insult was derived from the name of theologian and scholar John Duns Scotus by his apparently numerous enemies.

A dance.

WALTER
In faith, I will examine me this text
And see if by its hand its maker's traced.
Hark; here's the name of its rude author,
One Laurence Sellers, living in the north.   20
He dwelleth near a tavern, in and out
Reputed for the searing of beefsteak.

DONALD
Those be fine beefsteaks, Walter.

WALTER
Hold thy tongue, Donald; I've not said all.
The varlet is a youth whose father stands   25
A titan in the world of hired players,
A playwright, Arthur Digby Sellers call'd.
His plays renown'd throughout the continent,
Bulk of the series, Knave, and no light-weight.
How tragic that his son doth prove a dunce!   30
An north we proceed, once concluded be
The merriment of this performance piece—

DONALD
Then might we dine on beefsteaks, in and out?

WALTER
Hold thy tongue, Donald, I pray thee; thou art a great eater
of beef, and I believe that does harm to thy wit. Yea, we shall   35
brace the kid; he shall be o'er-push'd with certitude. We shall
take what moneys he hath not spent, and yea, we shall be near
the place of good repute, to feast on beefsteaks, have some ales
and merry jests. Our troubles be over, Knave.

Exeunt.

3 **corvette:** a small warship, smaller than a frigate; from the French *corvair*

13 **muse:** a source of inspiration. From the eponymous Greek goddesses who would spark the creation of art; for Walter, Sellers might have been most analogous to Calliope, muse of epic poetry, who inspired long narratives of great deeds and cultural heroes.

16 **orthography:** correct method of writing

A corvette.

SCENE 2

Outside a castle in the north. Enter THE KNAVE, WALTER,
and DONALD.

THE KNAVE
Alack! Regard this finest car without;
The child hath spent the bulk of money mine
On yon conveyance, like a corvette ship
To sail on simpler waters than I swim.

WALTER
Not so; the vehicle's but three or four   5
Per cent of all thy gains the villain seized,
Dependent on the trappings. Donald, hold;
We'll speak with young Laurence, and circle swift.
Ho, Squire Laurence! Reveal thyself and chat.

Enter LAURENCE SELLERS.

Thy father suffers problems with his health   10
And writes no more—a shame on it, say I,
For on a level personal his works
Were muse to me; I was a man to love
The early episodes birth'd of his quill.
Thou art a writer, Laurence, as I've read,   15
Though one of orthography correctèd.

He raises the document.

Thou art a lad of years mayhap fifteen,
At once a lad and coming to a man
Who's wise, I trust, to welcome not the law,
Constabulary actions being harsh.   20

21 **parchment:** thin material made from animal skin, used as a writing surface

23 **chattels:** goods, merchandise

27 **mewling:** crying or whimpering, as a baby

38 **impudence:** excessively bold or disrespectful behaviour

Home-work in progress.

Is this thy parchment, Laurence? Tell me true.
Is this thy parchment, Laurence? Tell me plain.

THE KNAVE
Be quick, Sir Walter! Ask of chattels bought.
Ask if that fine corvette without be his.

WALTER
Is this thy parchment, Laurence? Home-work thine?   25

THE KNAVE
We know that well, Sir Walter! His it be!
Whither the money, varlet, mewling spawn?

WALTER
Demand him nothing. What we know, we know.
From this time forth he never will speak word.
Hark, Laurence, hast thou studied of a place   30
Of Orient jungles?

THE KNAVE
Walter, prithee nay!

WALTER
Youth, thou art entering a world of pain.
We know this document is home-work thine,
And that thou stealest cars—   35

THE KNAVE
And moneys too!

WALTER
And moneys, and this is thy home-work, boy.
Wherefore silence? What impudence is this?
Thou art killing thy father, Laurence! O!

40 **This hath no end:** used in the conventional sense, but also to mean that there is no point or goal to be achieved in questioning Laurence further

45 **firk'st:** to beat or strike

Clown: comic relief character, often lower-class, though not necessarily a circus-style clown as we understand the term today. Clowns often existed outside the main plot and provided commentary or insight into the action; aside from traditionally garbed jesters, examples from Shakespeare include the gravediggers in *Hamlet* and the porter in *Macbeth*.

55 **shuffled off this mortal coil:** died. 'Mortal coil' refers to the collection of suffering and troubles that plague, or perhaps comprise, life on earth.

This hath no end; he never will speak word.   40
I take thy parchment back, and turn to plans
Of secondary contingence. Look well.
Behold thy car, the corvette, crimson-stain'd,
And see what befalls sinners evermore.

He raises his sword, and smites the car.

This befalleth when thou firk'st a stranger 'twixt the buttocks,   45
Laurence! Understand'st thou? Dost thou attend me? Seest thou
what happens, Laurence? Seest thou what happens, Laurence?
Seest thou what happens, Laurence, when thou firk'st a stranger
'twixt the buttocks?!

Enter CLOWN.

This be what befalleth, Laurence! This be what befalleth, Lau-   50
rence!

CLOWN
What hast thou wrought, thou wraith of province strange?
The corvette be my purchase yester-week;
Alas! My car, admired, baby mine.
My car hath shuffled off this mortal coil.   55

WALTER
Marry, an honest blunder; I knew it never thine.

CLOWN
I maketh thee to shuffle off this mortal coil, man! Nay, I'll
be revenged in proper recompense, suiting the punishment to
the action, the action to the punishment; I maketh thy car to
shuffle off this mortal coil!   60

The theatre of Jaques Treehorn: Treehorn, like Shakespeare, writes for his own specific company. Shakespeare started out as an actor before writing for the Lord Chamberlain's Men beginning in 1594, performing at The Theatre in Shoreditch and then moving to the Curtain Theatre three years later. In 1599, they constructed their own playhouse, the Globe. The business savvy of a well-compensated house playwright is reflected in the quality of Treehorn's estate.

7 **crack'd:** i.e., surrendered, owing to overwhelming emotional pressure

He raises his sword, and smites THE KNAVE's car.

THE KNAVE
No! Thou hast trespass'd wrongly; that be not Sir Walter's conveyance, but mine own!

CLOWN
I maketh thy car to shuffle off this mortal coil! I maketh thy
accursed car to shuffle off this mortal coil!

DONALD
Faith! I sit within, and cringe in fear;   65
What fools these mortals be that tarry here!

Exeunt.

SCENE 3

The theatre of JAQUES TREEHORN. Enter THE KNAVE.

THE KNAVE
Here I stand on quarters unfamiliar,
A pad of land of quality unspoil'd,
Having dined on beefsteak on the journey
In and out; and whereupon Sir Walter
Tender'd his apologies remorseful,   5
Hoping that I might have made it home,
Wond'ring still if Laurence may have crack'd.
Upon my homeward coming was I met
Most harshly by these ruffians unschool'd
Who've traffick'd in my house; I like them not.   10

Enter BLANCHE and WOO.

BLANCHE
Again we meet, Lebowski, who thou art;

14 **sprite:** spirit

20 **brew of whitest Russia:** the Knave may be suggesting, in jest, that he be served a then-unknown ambrosia of unsurpassed perfection

21 **as fair York's rose:** i.e., as white as the heraldic rose of the House of York

24 **dumb-show:** a pantomime act

28 **mechanicals:** manual labourers

'Whitest Russia'

And yea, we know of which Lebowski art
Thy deadbeat frame.

WOO
So do attend, O sprite;
Thou dealest not with fools this wicked night.   15

Exeunt BLANCHE and WOO. Flourish. Enter JAQUES
TREEHORN.

JAQUES TREEHORN
Good Knave, my thanks for travels thou hast made;
By Jaques Treehorn I am called in name.
I bid thee welcome to my humble home
And beg thee take a bev'rage of thy choice.

THE KNAVE
The brew of whitest Russia I would sip,   20
As fair York's rose. How fares thy working trade?

JAQUES TREEHORN
A playwright and theatre-man am I,
With tendrils dipp'd in lakes of many stripes,
In printed word, in dumb-show and in court.

THE KNAVE
Which be 'Log Jamming'?   25

JAQUES TREEHORN
Thou readest my regret;
The playhouse is a place of disrepair.
When rude mechanicals may gather nights
To play in interludes most amateur,
We cut the very wheat from our fair crop   30
And make poor sport of spectacle and tale,

38 **compass:** accomplish, bring about

43 **read . . . manually:** by hand. The Knave may be affirming his literacy here; he can read, and write or copy text by hand, and thus has no need for the dramatic wonders of Treehorn's theatre.

44 **rub:** obstacle

A beaver picture.

With no more tears in the performing of't.
Thy brain hath in the function of its power
The zone where faith is firmly fix'd in love,
Richer than all thy tribe in other parts.   35

THE KNAVE
On thee, mayhap.

JAQUES TREEHORN
The brightest heaven of invention
May yet compass wonders fit for devils
In greatest fair effects of future hopes.
Such plays may well transport us all beyond   40
This ignorant present.

THE KNAVE
Faith, an excellent dream;
But I still read Ben Jonson manually.

JAQUES TREEHORN
Ay, there's the rub. I pray thee, Knave, to hear
The purpose of my night's invitation   45
As brought thee to my seat. Where's Bonnie fair?

THE KNAVE
O irony; I thought that thou couldst know.

JAQUES TREEHORN
My mind is slate and sky-dark; the lady
Only ran off to flee her debt to me,
A bond, a sizable bond.   50

THE KNAVE
But she ran not!

JAQUES TREEHORN
I know thy troubles, Knave, the tangled web
Woven upon the practice to deceive.
An thou robbest her husband, I care not.
How goes the world, that I am thus encounter'd   55
With clamorous demands of broken bonds
And the detention of long-since-due debts?

THE KNAVE
Well spoke; but sir, there many facets be.
The parties of interest are of scope
And multitude in number. What's for me,   60
What of the Knave, if he retains thy gold?

JAQUES TREEHORN
The tenth part of the plunder shall be thine;
But drink thou from thy goblet, ere it warms.

THE KNAVE
I'll drink your health, good Jaques, as a friend
For greatly is thy jib-cut most admired.   65
The Knave carouses to thy fortune, Treehorn.
But hark! O venom! What betides my drink,
That makes me swoon? The drink. I am poison'd.
The treacherous White Russian in my hand.

He falls.

And all the Knave e'er wanted was his rug   70
As spoken of, which tied the room together.
Look sharp! Darkness overtakes the Knave,
Of blacker shade than cattle's secret parts
On moonless nights in Devonshire. I fall.

---

8 **liked my jerkin not:** probably an insult related to social class. The jerkin, as compared to the doublet, was workman's wear for the middle and lower classes, and unsuitable attire for a garden party. The constable may have reacted to the Knave's ignoble fashion in addition to his behaviour. For more information, consult Janet Winter and Carolyn Savoy, *Elizabethan Costuming for the Years 1550–1580,* 2nd edition (Oakland, CA: Other Times Publications, 1987).

9 **beach community:** probably Dover, a port town known primarily for the sheer white cliffs that overlook its shoreline but also for its strict constabulary

10 **eagles:** a reference to the eagle as a hated symbol of the Holy Roman Empire and German fascists

17 **queen:** the Knave's tacit admission that by lying with him and wearing his clothes, she has become his queen, i.e., become his wife and in charge of running his home

17 **special ladies:** a term of endearment indicating a woman's position of great respect within the social order

'And eagles gazed upon with every eye'

It hath no bottom, not this apparition;   75
I drop to view the state of my condition.

Exeunt severally.

SCENE 4

THE KNAVE's house. Enter THE KNAVE.

THE KNAVE
I have had a most rare vision. I have had a dream past the wit
of man to say what dream it was. Methought I waked to find
I could be bound in a satchel of infinite space, only to be over-
come by a summer's cloud, to throw myself to heaven, to have
my mind scrape upon the smirch'd complexion of the sky, and   5
tear it thus. Most peculiar.
Then was I found by night-watch constable,
Who liked my jerkin not, and told me thus,
And cast me from his beach community.
And eagles gazed upon with every eye;   10
And O, I hate the cursèd eagles, man.

Enter MAUDE.

It is my lady friend, it is my love.

MAUDE
Come, thou spirit that tends on mortal thoughts,
Come lie with me under the greenwood tree
And know the heat of a luxurious bed   15
And in our faults by lies we'll flatter'd be.

THE KNAVE
My Maude is now the queen of special ladies,
Attired in a robe that is mine own.

23–25 **Port Huron . . . Seattle:** possibly settlements in the New World, the details of which have been lost to history

41 **claims it as his crop:** Lebowski pretends that his inheritance was produced by his own achievement. Shakespeare, an eldest surviving son whose own father left behind only financial problems, apparently took a dim view of inheritances: he left his wife, Anne Hathaway, only his second-best bed.

They kiss, and lay down.

MAUDE
Speak of thyself, O Geoffrey, while we sleep.

THE KNAVE
Let me present my life-time as a Knave,   20
Though little stands to tell; but tarry soft.
I'd tell thee how, in youth, I did author
A statement in Port Huron, ere the turn
When it emerged in compromised draft.
Or how, in fair Seattle, I and six   25
Were charged conspirators against the King;
Yea, that was me; and sixfold other men.
I turn'd attention briefly to the lute
And fife, and tour'd with men of speed and sound,
Who asses were; now I do nothing much,   30
Mayhap a bit of this, a bit of that.
I play at ninepins on the village green
And ride horseback, and think on wilder days.
My house is sack'd by Jaques Treehorn's men
Who thought to seek thy father's money here; 35
A case of great complexity we glimpse,
With many ins and outs, as I have said.

MAUDE arranges herself upon the floor.

MAUDE
The money's the foundation's, not the man's.
My father hath no money of his own;
The wealth was his inheritance to tend   40
And pompously he claims it as his crop.
O vanity of Father! Fierce extremes

53 **I'll live unpartner'd:** Maude's refusal to marry is tremendously unorthodox. That she has secured power over men while remaining unmarried could be a Shakespearean parody of Queen Elizabeth. Because of this, and her general audacity, Maude's role would likely have been costumed with red hair.

58–59 **govern'd by humours:** swept up by excitement and new thoughts

Marriage.

Of personality he built so as to seem
The wide world's emperor; and hence the whore,
So purchased as to sate his glory-thirst.   45

THE KNAVE
Wherefore thy strange position on the floor?

MAUDE
I crave a young conception in my womb,
And seat me thus to better take thy seed.

THE KNAVE
But I a father poorly made would be!

MAUDE
Nay, I seek no partner in this babe;   50
I love thee not, therefore pursue me not.
Our comedy ends not with marriage-bed,
I'll live unpartner'd, and unbotherèd.

THE KNAVE
Marry! Then thou wouldst have a child of bastard blood, without a father, as thou thyself might well have wish'd to have no   55
father; but now I think upon thy father, and lo, new stuff doth
come to light breaking forth. My thinking on thy sorry case
had become most up-tighten'd, and I am altogether govern'd by
humours. Quickly, away! I must to Sir Walter.

Exeunt.

SCENE 5

The road. Enter THE KNAVE.

THE KNAVE
I wait upon the coming of Sir Walter

4 **Evensong:** evening prayer

10 **dirk:** a Scottish dagger or small sword. Brother Seamus is boasting of his speed and undetectability.

11 **lady friend:** a term of endearment for a woman, used in informal courtship. Contrast with 'special lady.'

15 **swell her womb:** conceive

19 **wand'ring daughters:** Shakespeare's plots occasionally featured young women who were unaccountably bold for the norms of the time. Examples include Rosalind and Celia from *As You Like It* 'wandering' in Arden forest, and Cordelia, the only daughter of King Lear who refused to flatter him.

21 **Moorhead:** unknown, probably a peasants' settlement in the North

Monks, location unknown.

Who, on my dispatch, flew him to emerge
That we might charge Lebowski in his guilt
And right these monstrous wrongs ere Evensong.

        Enter BROTHER SEAMUS.

Who's there?   5

BROTHER SEAMUS
Be still! I'll harm thy person not.
'Tis I, the Brother Seamus, Irish monk—
A man the finer having seen thee work,
A stalking spy for private clientele,
A dirk; a man who seeketh for to find.   10

THE KNAVE
That's well; but keep thee from my lady friend.

BROTHER SEAMUS
I never tempted her with word too large;
I knew her not thy special lady fair.

THE KNAVE
She's not my special lady but my friend;
I help'd her swell her womb. Who hired thee?   15
Art thou a servant of Lebowski state,
Or Jaques Treehorn, or some goblin damn'd?

BROTHER SEAMUS
I travel on the charge of sons of knights,
A job of wand'ring daughters from the north.
The lady Bonnie's falsely bonny bred.   20
Her name be Faun, a girl of Moorhead born,
Whose parents wish her back with broken hearts;
This past twelvemonth she fled the family farm
And I'm to show her paintings of the land.

25 **paint:** indicating that Bonnie is a painted lady, or whore. See Act 1, Scene 4.

27 **pastoral:** bucolic, rural

29 **steward:** caretaker

38 **vows of Sabbath pure:** the commandment to keep holy the Sabbath day, i.e., *shomer Shabbos*

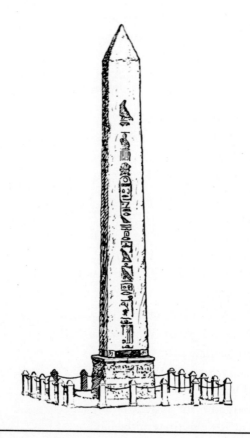

THE KNAVE
The lady's love for paint is plain to see,   25
But she hath seen Karl Hungus, and is like
To not exchange it for pastoral life.

BROTHER SEAMUS
Alack the day! O fairest damsel lost!
It is a false steward that steals a master's daughter.
Mayhap we might our slim resources pool,   30
Exchange our facts in noble courtesy,
In friendship and professionality.

THE KNAVE
Nay, for thou art none the finer man.
Away, sirrah; my ride approacheth nigh.
And stay away from special lady mine,   35
Or lady friend, as I would have it writ.

    Exit BROTHER SEAMUS; enter WALTER (with dog).

WALTER
Thy messenger decreed emergency
And so I broke my vows of Sabbath pure,
For this the holy day of resting be
For gentle Jews; now state thy purpose, Knave.   40

THE KNAVE
We must away to old Lebowski's house
To press him on the matter of this case.
We botch'd his bargain with the villains vile
That night, and in his anger, though he yell'd,
He visited no harm upon my head   45
Nor render'd my weak body punishèd.

47 **catharsis:** a Greek term (from *kathairein,* to purify or purge) signifying emotional cleansing. In his *Poetics,* Aristotle defined the function of tragedy as a catharsis of pity and fear. Shakespeare's familiarity with Aristotle is unknown, though his tragedies do conform to some of the *Poetics'* requirements for drama, such as including a flawed protagonist.

49 **afoot:** in progress, in motion

55 **no true gold:** 'fool's gold'; the Knave is indicating he has been treated as a fool

56 **accord:** harmony or agreement; the Knave was not given the money Lebowski agreed to provide

59 **Methinks:** i.e., it appears to me

69 **Papists:** Catholics

WALTER
Mayhaps the gentle soul's catharsis lay
In shouting at thee.

THE KNAVE
Nay; a game's afoot.
He knows I am a fool; I do agree,   50
But why wouldst he me charge to save his wife?
Methinks the man despised his lady fair
And plotted ill to profit from her loss
And in his sinning sought to make a show.
I'll tell thee this; he gave me no true gold   55
Nor jewels, nor any treasure of accord
To toss the thieves; nor effort has he made
To have of me the haul from him I stole.
Methinks the money that we thought was lost
Was never thus, but weight like laundries thine: 60
Our ringer was a ringer for the same
In odious Lebowski's rotten game.

WALTER
O double falsehood of distressed lovers!
I mark thee, and pay tribute to thy wits,
Deduction noble made, but all the same   65
Must query quick the nature of this crime
That leads me out of doors on Sabbath eve.

THE KNAVE
Sir Walter, prithee cease; thou art no Jew.
Of Papists born in Poland was thy line.

70 **converted:** changed one's religion. Given the rampant and state-supported persecution of Jews, an Elizabethan audience would have understood Walter's choice to turn Jewish as a terrible risk, and thus an act of supreme, even suicidal, devotion to Cynthia.

75 **divorce:** to end a marriage; an option readily available under Jewish law even in Elizabethan times, though much more difficult under English and Church law. Not until the Matrimonial Causes Act of 1857 was the governance of divorce moved from the ecclesiastical Court of Arches to the civil courtroom.

81 **rock:** i.e., rock-solid, steadfast, unmoving

84 **synagogue:** Jewish house of prayer; from the Greek *synagein*, to bring together

87 **Moses:** from the Book of Exodus, the most respected prophet in Judaism

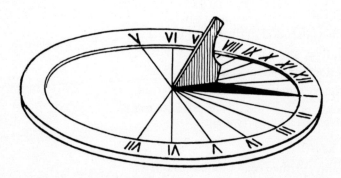

WALTER
Thou knowest I converted ere I wed   70
The Lady Cynthia.

THE KNAVE
But that is past;
Five twelvemonths cross'd the sky since thou were wed.

WALTER
'Tis true, I have in oath and court of law
Made a divorce betwixt Cynthia and me,   75
But doth equivocation turn a heart?
When justice calls a Jew into the court
Must not a Jew emerge? Is he anew?
May I no more of libraries borrow,
Or push my cart, or be my selfsame man?   80
The Hebrew turns not Christian; he is rock.

THE KNAVE
Thy sickness for fair Cynthia is sad;
Thou carest for her cur, though are not wed,
And still her synagogue thou dost attend.
Thou livest in the most accursèd past.   85

WALTER
Forsooth! Three thousand years of history,
Traditions beauteous from Moses on:
Thou speakest damnèd truth, and speakest best,
I am a man to live in bygone past!
But let's away; the big Lebowski waits,   90
And fate rewards no man who hesitates.

Exeunt.

TWO GENTLEMEN
OF
LEBOWSKI

ACT 5

2 **in her cups:** drunk
2 **brave:** admirably
10 **came . . . to wive:** undertook the search to get married

ACT 5

SCENE 1

LEBOWSKI's castle. Flourish. Enter THE KNAVE, WALTER,
and BONNIE.

THE KNAVE
Look well on Bonnie, something like the sun.
She hath been in her cups, and singing brave
Converting all her sounds of woe into
Hey-nonny-nonny; hark.

BONNIE
Long live the meadows! Let us have a song.   5

[sings]

'But when I came to Lebowski estate
With hey, ho, the fountain doth rain
I used my car to batter the gate
For the Knave abideth every day.
And when I came, alas! to wive   10
With hey, ho, the fountain doth rain
By swaggering could I constantly thrive
For the Knave abideth every day.'

Exit BONNIE; enter BRANDT.

16 **palmer:** holy pilgrim

23 **Beshrew me:** as earlier. Note the additional pun that the big Lebowski's 'shrew' (Bonnie) has returned.

27 **curst:** crossed, shrewish. Or possibly 'cursed.'

31 **bolting-hutch:** a bin, tub, or receptacle for meal or flour

32 **knotty-pated:** block-headed

A toad.

BRANDT
Thine eyes deceive thee not; the lady lives,
No longer vanishèd; what's lost is found.   15
She left to see the palmer at the springs
And told no man that she would go away.
Good Knave, I pray thee, bother not my lord,
For he is angry; prithee, who is this?

WALTER
I'll tell thee who I am; a veteran, I,   20
A soldier of the honour-giving field
Of mire and muck and fens; we'll have thy lord.

Exit BRANDT; enter LEBOWSKI on his cart.

LEBOWSKI
Beshrew me! That my door be darken'd thus
By this foul cheat who found me not my bride.

THE KNAVE
Whither the money, Lebowski?   25

WALTER
A thousand pounds from young achievers robb'd!
O rude and vilest villain! Coward curst!
A most notable coward of no quality
Whose tongue outvenoms all the worms of Nile.
Thou art as loathsome as a toad, thou vice,   30
A bolting-hutch of beastliness, thou mite,
Thou clay-brained guts, thou knotty-pated fool!

LEBOWSKI
Thou hast thy history and I have mine.
I say that ye hath stole my thousand pounds.

36 **paroquet:** parakeet. In addition to insulting Lebowski's intelligence and substantiality, the Knave is also calling him unsanitary, spreading foul droppings and disease.

43 **tallow:** cattle fat rendered into a hard lump

45 **Tush, tush:** an expression of mild admonition or reproof

WALTER
O wound! I wouldst not dream to filch thy wealth.   35

THE KNAVE
Thou art a villain, human paroquet!
Thou thought thy wife vanish'd, and thought it well!
Thou hadst met me and thought my mettle right
To be thy pawn, a man of ill repute
Who circles not amidst men of good square,   40
That thou might use to shuffle gold about.

LEBOWSKI
Well? Art thou not a man of no regard,
A greasy tallow husk of failèd flesh?

THE KNAVE
Perchance.

WALTER
Tush, tush; let's speak of him instead.   45
An infinite and endless liar, he.
A curse shall light upon the limbs of men.
I've seen my share of spines a-damagèd;
This sinner stands to walk most capably.
Stand now, O villain! Up upon thy feet!   50

LEBOWSKI
Step back, I prithee; stay not close to me.

WALTER
Up, so! How is't? Feel you your legs? You stand.
I bid thee walk afoot, if thou be man!

He casts LEBOWSKI from his cart; LEBOWSKI falls.

55 **sea-legs:** the ability to walk steadily on a ship; Lebowski has none. Walter's aggression toward him, ironically, will not stand.

---

1 **armour'd conflict:** a battle on land
9 **Sir Charles:** probably a slight to a historical knight or peer of Walter, probably French. Candidates include suspected witch Charles I, Count of Nevers; greedy Charles of Valois; or the aptly nicknamed Charles the Bad. Anglo-French relations in Shakespeare's day were calmer than usual, in light of the Spanish threat, but memories remained long.

'War in far-flung jungles, as my friends
Did die face-down in mire and muck and fens!'

THE KNAVE
O, he hath fallen!

WALTER
'Pon my life, I might have sworn he had his sea-legs.   55

THE KNAVE
Thou art a fool and of thee I despair.
We must away; let's help him to his chair.

They set him back into his cart. Exeunt.

SCENE 2

The bowling green. Enter THE KNAVE and WALTER.

WALTER
No doubt we'll see some armour'd conflict yet,
Some battle fare unto the morning's war.
But fighting in the arid desert be
A diff'ring beast from skirmishes as I
Experienced in jungles canopied.   5
That was a soldier's war, by Jove, whereas
This thing shall be as cake, and warm within.
I had me but my bow and quiver set,
No heavy horse; 'twas I and good Sir Charles,
'Twere face to face and eye to eye opposed.   10

Enter DONALD.

That be combat, forsooth; the man in black,
An adversary worthy on the mount.

DONALD
Walter, pray, who be attired in black?

15 **eaters of the fig:** foreigners; nothing to be afraid of

16 **bareback:** without the protection of a saddle

23 **laughable:** provoking derisive laughter. The coinage of this word is often attributed to Shakespeare's *The Merchant of Venice*.

32 **Greek fire:** an incendiary compound developed by the Byzantines to burn on water

Greek fire.

WALTER
Hold thy tongue, Donald—I speak of men,
Not eaters of the fig in motley clad   15
Affirming to ride bareback in reverse.
These men be none of worth, and I'll have none.

Enter QUINCE and O'BRIEN.

QUINCE
Thou dunce, thou varlet; whence this day of rest?
To bowl on Sabbath matters not to me
And fools me not; it may deceive the leaguesmen,   20
But none of woman born fools Joshua.
Thy games of mind are fit for childrens' spoils,
And laughable; my act is but delay'd,
For if I will not have thee Saturday
I'll surely have my way with thee mid-week.   25
This Wednesday thou and I a-courting go;
Think well on it!

Exeunt QUINCE and O'BRIEN.

WALTER
By my life, he cracks.

THE KNAVE
Think not on him till Wednesday, for the game;
Our worries stretch to higher fruit than he.   30
Look well: the nihilists approach our green
And bring Greek fire to our quiet lot.
My burning car doth hotly scorch the earth!
The weary moon hath shone upon our park
And lit the burnt husk of my fiery car!   35

40 **ninnies:** simpletons or foolish people. Possibly derived from 'innocent.'

45 **in any case:** possibly a nod to Walter's prior use of a ringer

50 **cabbage-fed:** low-class; only able to afford cabbage for meals

51 **consort:** a romantic companion

52 **a thousandfold:** i.e., a thousand times over

Alarums. Enter OLIVER and the NIHILISTS.

It hath finally been done. They made my car to shuffle off the
mortal coil.

OLIVER
Money buys lands, Lebowski, and wives are slain by fate; we'll
be poisonous and kill thy forlorn queen.

THE KNAVE
Ye have not th'accursed girl, ye ninnies! We know ye never had   40
so comely a maid.

DONALD
Be these the tyrants, Sir Walter?

WALTER
Nay! These nihilists be, and none to fear.
But few of any sort, and none of name.

OLIVER
We would have the money in any case, else we visit much griev-   45
ous damage upon your persons.

WALTER
Nay! Thou hast no hostage to avenge:
Thy ransom there is none but we shall pay!
We'll not obey that know not ransom's rules,
Ye cabbage-fed foul sons of ugly curs!   50

FIRST NIHILIST
Verily did his consort give her toe
In hopes of seeking gold a thousandfold.

61 **empty wares:** i.e., goods of no value
62 **quarrel:** argument, but also the ammunition used in a crossbow
64 **fly:** flee, depart
66 **what minor gold:** i.e., whatever small amount of money
67 **doublets:** men's buttoned jackets, often padded and decorated
68 **Fie:** an interjection indicating dismissal, annoyance or contempt

SECOND NIHILIST
It is not fair; 'tis foul but never fair!

WALTER
And wherefore 'fair', when ye be nihilists?
Wherefore the nihilist weeps and cries for 'fair'?   55
Thy dispute is of infants, weeping woes,
Spoke as an idiot, full of sound and fury,
Believing in nothing.

THE KNAVE
Walter, pray be still.
Good nihilist, the money never was;   60
Yon big Lebowski gave me empty wares,
So take thy quarrel up his lordship's way.

WALTER
And I request my breeches ere we part!

DONALD
In sooth, I fear they'll hurt us ere we fly.

WALTER
Not so! They cowards be, and amateurs.   65

OLIVER
'Tis well; we'll take what minor gold ye have
In doublets thine, and all's well that ends well.

WALTER
Fie on thee! What's mine is ever mine.

THE KNAVE
Nay, let's end cheaply; four sixpence I hold.

74 **pity my case:** i.e., have mercy on me
79 **haters of Jewry:** anti-Semites. In Elizabethan England, practically
    a synonym for 'everyone.'

'We bleed on both sides'

DONALD
And eighteen further in my saddlebag.   70

OLIVER
The gold, anon! Or I'll be set on thee.

WALTER
What's mine is mine; lay on, nihilist,
And damn'd be he that nine-toed woman kiss'd!

They fight.

DONALD
Alas, my lord, I cannot fight; for God's sake, pity my case. I
shall never be able to fight a blow. O Lord, my heart!   75

OLIVER

[to WALTER]

I firk thee! I firk thee! Verily I firk thee!

WALTER
We bleed on both sides. Have at you now!

OLIVER
I firk thee!

They fight, and the NIHILISTS die.

WALTER
Ever thus to haters of Jewry!

DONALD falls.

DONALD
O, I am slain!   80

---

3 **fields Elysian:** the final resting place of heroes or men of great virtue; from Greek mythology
4 **urn:** in Shakespeare's day, cremation carried theological implications. The Catholic Church frowned on the practice, viewing it as denying the possibility of resurrection, but the Church of England was less restrictive. Cremation was also employed for practical reasons, such as disposing of large numbers of bodies after a battle; perhaps Walter is remembering Donald as a fallen soldier.

THE KNAVE
Hark, hark! Man down! Walter, they shot him thus!

WALTER
No, Knave; no bowstring ever arrow left.
His heart is weak; a heart easily daunted.
Hear, hear how dying Sir Donald doth groan!

DONALD
O, I die, Lebowski;   85
The potent fervour quite o'er-crows my spirit.
Thou hast my dying voice; the rest is silence.

He dies.

WALTER
Alas, sweet friend! Now we shall mourn for thee,
O could our mourning ease our misery!

Exeunt, carrying DONALD.

SCENE 3

*A churchyard. Enter THE KNAVE, WALTER, and a
GRAVEDIGGER carrying a spade and a pickaxe.*

GRAVEDIGGER
I greet ye, an ye are the men bereaved,
And mark ye well to escort the remains
Of your late friend to fields Elysian.
Look to the urn; let's settle now the fee.

WALTER
The urn is well, but we demand it not;   5
We seek to send the ashes scatter-shot.

9 **quest:** inquest; an investigation into the surroundings of a death in the hope new stuff will come to light

10 **receptacle:** a container, from the Latin *receptaculum*

---

2 **glooming:** from the Middle English *gloumen,* to become dark

8 **envious:** malicious

A gravedigger.

GRAVEDIGGER
'Twas said, but ashes must be given ye
In a receptacle of quality.
'Tis coroner's quest law; will it suffice?
For this receptacle be humbly priced.   10

THE KNAVE
Might men of modest means who need thine urn
Be borrowers of it till our return?

WALTER
Sorrow and grief hath vanquish'd not our powers;
We are not saplings weak in tragic hours.
Come, good Knave; to market we shall send,   15
A jar we'll buy to honour fallen friends.

Exeunt.

SCENE 4

*A cliffside. Enter THE KNAVE and WALTER, with a jar of
clay.*

WALTER
Words, words, words. I'll speak.
A glooming peace this morning with it brings:
The sun, for sorrow, will not show his head.
We come here to have talk of these sad things;
Of Donald, who we loved, and who bowlèd.   5
He was a straight and true bowler, and a virtuous man. He was
of our sort, a man who loved the woods free from peril of the
envious court. And he loved bowling well. He knew the pebbles
on the hungry beach. And yea, he was a bowler most avid. And

21 **sweet prince:** used here as a term of endearment. Walter may also be reflecting on Donald's relative youth.

25 **crackèd cheeks:** puffed-out cheeks. Maps and illustrations of the period depicted winds in the form of clouds blowing over the land and possibly on freshly-painted toes.

29 **travesty:** exaggerated, debased, or grotesque parody

a fair friend, who never can be old. He died as did so many of   10
his generation, ere his time. In Thy wisdom, Lord, Thou didst
take him, as Thou took so many bright flowering young men, i'
the jungles of the Orient. These young men gave their lives, and
Donald too; Donald who loved to play at ninepins.
And so, Sir Donald, in fairest accordance   15
With what your wishes last well might have been,
We make commitment of your last remains
To the deep bosom of the ocean buried,
A peaceful progress to the ocean, which
You loved so well. Now cracks a bowler's heart.   20

He scatters the ashes.

Good night, sweet prince,
And flights of angels sing thee to thy rest.

THE KNAVE
But soft! The sorrow's wind hath strewn the ash
And cover'd me in that we came to spill.

WALTER
Alack! Blown winds and crackèd cheeks! Raged! Blown!   25

THE KNAVE
Thou art an ass! A stupefying ass!

WALTER
Apologies.

THE KNAVE
Thou hast ruin'd all again!
Thou makest all a travesty of pain!

33 **deadly-standing:** death-dealing. The Knave is also referring to Walter's war story as his 'standing,' or constant, refrain.

---

1 **ales of oat-brew:** beers. In general, Elizabethan-era beer was weaker and flatter than today's product, with a bitter taste often masked with flavourings like berries or pepper.

6 **rent:** tore

6 **fall:** death

WALTER
'Twas accident! I meant not for the breeze.　　　　　30

THE KNAVE
Thy statement, man! The stuff on jungle war.
What signifies thy foreign conflict here?
What signifies thy deadly-standing speech?
I'll have no more; thou art a raging fool.

WALTER
I stand before thee tainted with remorse, and beg thy mercy; I　35
am overcome. A pox upon't, Knave; let us play at ninepins.

Exeunt.

SCENE 5

*The tavern near the bowling green. Enter THE KNAVE and
MISTRESS QUICKLY.*

THE KNAVE
I'll have two ales of oat-brew, hostess fair.

MISTRESS QUICKLY
Anon. My fondest wishes for the sport
In tourney celebrated on the morrow.

THE KNAVE
I give thee thanks.

MISTRESS QUICKLY
And I thee sadder thoughts;　　　　　　　　　　5
It rent my heart to read of Donald's fall.

11 **semifinal games:** two matches in the penultimate round of a tournament. Also, perhaps, the Chorus's acknowledgement that the Knave's team without Donald is only half-complete.

13 **gutters:** troughs dug to carry away rainwater and garbage

A game of bowls.

THE KNAVE
'Tis well; sometimes thou exits in pursuit
Of bear, and sometimes he doth pursue thee.

Enter CHORUS.

But here's the man of whom I had these words!
I wonder'd if he'd cross my path again.   10

CHORUS
I dare not miss the semifinal games.
How fares my good and noble friend the Knave?

THE KNAVE
Thou knowest; strikes and gutters, ups and downs.

CHORUS
Marry, be of ease, O gentle Knave;
I know thou wilt.   15

THE KNAVE
Thou know'st. The Knave abideth.

Exeunt all but CHORUS.

5 **shadows:** spirits, but also actors, who exist only as representations of the characters they portray

21 **catch thee down the trail:** i.e., see you again in the future. The Chorus paints *Two Gentlemen of Lebowski* as a fairy tale, encouraging us to forget the grim undercurrents of the story (deception, vandalism, kidnapping, theft, and Donald's senseless death) and embrace the cycle of life. By giving us his promise to rejoin us, the Chorus assures us that all will be well. He ends with a statement that the story is over, signaling a request for the audience's applause.

EPILOGUE

CHORUS

'The Knave abideth'. I dare speak not for thee, but this maketh
me to be of good comfort; I deem it well that he be out there,
the Knave, being of good ease for we sinners. I hope he proveth
well in the tourney.

If we shadows have offended,   5
Think but this and all is mended,
That you have but slumbered here
While these visions did appear.
And all wrapp'd up be this idle theme,
A noble and a pretty story-dream   10
Made me laugh to overtake the band,
Parts, in sooth; and others less so scann'd.
I did not like to see Sir Donald go,
But then, the fellow wise is like to know
That on the way's a little Lebowski   15
Perpetuating human comedy
Down through the generations; westward on,
Across the sands of time—but heed my song;
I ramble yet, and so must take my leave,
And hope thou liked my tale of the good Knave.   20
If we be friends, I'll catch thee down the trail
And we shall share sarsaparilla ale.
For never was a story of more glee
Than this of Geoffrey and the Big Lebowski.

THE END

AFTERWORD

THE REST IS SILENCE

"The plays remain the outward limit of human achievement . . .
They abide beyond the end of the mind's reach."
—Harold Bloom, *Shakespeare: The Invention of the Human*

Hamlet had his question and I had mine: "What if"—pause for effect—"William Shakespeare wrote *The Big Lebowski*?"

I suppose I owe you an explanation.

The summer of 2009 was a magical time to be a Bardolator. Visionary director Julie Taymor's film of *The Tempest* was in postproduction. Noted Shakespearean actor Brian Blessed was making plans to explore outer space while boisterously shouting in iambic pentameter. Academy Award nominee Anne Hathaway was playing Viola in *Twelfth Night*. And the failing economy meant more time for reading instead of gainful employment or the trials of home ownership.

My own plans were less ambitious: chill with friends, get a little writing done. Panic about being in my late twenties and not having done anything with my life.

Although I did catch *Twelfth Night*. Great show. Hathaway signed my program afterward, took a picture with me. Laughed at my dumb joke about her name. Big fan here.

Then glorious summer blazed out, winter came, and I was discontent.

A few weeks later, there I was, bedecked in my finest bathrobe. Typing like a madman at two o'clock on a cold Sunday morning, with a Shakespeare concordance at my side and a half-liter of Coke Zero acid-frying my innards.

I can't explain why I thought it was a good idea. I'm not sure I thought, period. Bloggers, fans, and cultured types of every stripe ask what made me do it. I wish I knew. It just kind of happened.

Someone always brings up the authorship question: Did Shakespeare write all of his plays? I demur. Honestly, I don't care who wrote them. Why should I? So what if it was Kit Marlowe? Does that help me get through the day?

Instead, I'd like you to join me on an imaginative adventure. A voyage of consciousness, of the mind. The only kind of journey worth taking.

London. The tail end of the Elizabethan era. A contingent from the Globe Theatre attends an extraordinary new play.

The audience for *The Big Lebowski* is small but appreciative. The group pours out praising the inventive staging, the idiosyncratic characters, the marvelous dances. Only William Shakespeare remains quiet, kicking a piece of litter down the road. He's seen something of himself up on that stage.

He becomes inspired. He swipes the prompter's notes from the theater company and decides he's going to write his own version. *Two Gentlemen of Lebowski,* he calls it, and he knocks out the first draft in a weekend. He cackles to himself, shows all his actor friends, starts figuring out which part will go to Richard Burbage and which to Will Kempe. And he finds that the more time he spends with the work, the more he wonders how anyone but he wrote something so Shakespearean.

This is my contention: If *The Big Lebowski* had premiered in 1598, Shakespeare would have ripped it off by 1603.

It's not so hard to believe. The vast majority of Shakespeare's plays (the bulk of the series, if you will) can be linked to prior sources: history, classic stories, even the original work of other writers.

Romeo and Juliet was based on a pair of all-too-real doomed lovers, celebrated in a poem by Arthur Brooke and a short story by William Painter. *Hamlet* may well have its roots in a lost Thomas Kyd play from the previous decade. *The Taming of the Shrew* stole a subplot from the poet Ludovico Ariosto. *Othello* came from a short story by Cinthio; Shakespeare's contribution was partially a rewrite and partially a translation into Elizabethan English. (Why someone would do that, who can say.)

In Shakespeare's simpler, happier, plague-ridden times, plots and ideas were freely shared and adapted and reworked. Shakespeare thrived in an entertainment industry obsessed with remakes, adaptations, and mashups—just like Hollywood today. No wonder they say his stories are timeless.

But the beauty of Shakespeare was never in the plot alone. To think of *The Big Lebowski* only in terms of its narrative of toes and marmots and ringers is to lose sight of the forest for the trees. The real beauty is in the language, the wonderful characters, the text from which springs one memorable quote after another. Shakespeare regularly thumbed his nose at complex plots and thorny details: he waffles on Hamlet's age, fudges the geography in *The Winter's Tale,* wraps up loose ends with magic fairies and impromptu weddings, and hurls about wacky coincidences with sitcom-level abandon. That's life. That's why he would have loved the Dude's story. He knew what was important.

The facts are these: (1) William Shakespeare was unquestionably the greatest writer who ever lived. (2) He loved a good dick joke. *The Big Lebowski* is certainly a piece of art, worthy of study and intelligent criticism, but it's also obsessed with the status of one's Johnson and legendary for its profanity. The clash of high and low culture is quintessentially Shakespearean as well, and the groundlings who giggled at "country matters" and "Faith, her privates we" in *Hamlet* are treated to a host of lowbrow hijinks in *Lebowski,* with its merry misadventures of roguish rascals chasing fast cash and drunken sport. We can easily imagine an Elizabethan Dude and Walter lost in some enchanted forest, cussin' along the way.

And the Dude fits into a glorious tradition of lazy, cheery scamps in literature. One can hardly think of Shakespeare's jovial, iconoclastic, dissolute genius Falstaff without wondering how he might enjoy White Russians or bowling. In *Shakespeare: The Invention of the Human,* Harold Bloom asserts, "It is the comprehensiveness of Falstaff's consciousness that puts him beyond us." He goes on: "I hear a great wit, but also an authentic sage, destroying illusions . . . rather in the mode of certain great poets who were not exactly wholesome and productive citizens." The Knave abideth, indeed.

"*Lebowski* is a bit like a Shakespeare comedy, if only in

the light-hearted sense that it celebrates life and love," observe J. M. Tyree and Ben Walters in their BFI Film Classics study of *The Big Lebowski*. Indeed, the film hews so close to classic Shakespearean comic devices that it verges on parody. It's a comedy of errors of mistaken identity, narrow escapes, and wise fools. The refined establishment against the wilder fringes of civilization. A little slapstick. Even cross-dressing gets a sly nod when Maude dons her future lover's robe, slyer still when one recalls that Shakespeare's Maude would have been played by a boy. All it's missing is twins.

Like many dramatists of his day, Shakespeare often employed a prologue and/or an epilogue. The role would be assayed by a character or an outside narrator; occasionally Shakespeare would blur the two for artistic effect and/or metatheatrical comment. (Our appreciation of Rosalind's direct address in *As You Like It*, for instance, depends in part on our recognition of the actor's identity. Sam Elliott, anyone?) Consulting *A Study of the Prologue and Epilogue in English Literature, from Shakespeare to Dryden* by G. S. Bower, we learn that costume was a key element of identifying a character "not known otherwise than by his style and title of 'The Prologue.'" We can conclude, then, that Shakespeare dug his prologue's style.

Every kid suffering through middle school English gets the fun little handout about the words and phrases that the Bard invented. As Bernard Levin famously pointed out, we're always quoting Shakespeare. What's more, Shakespeare was always quoting himself. Witness his use of the "rain it raineth" song, first in *Twelfth Night* and later in *King Lear*. Notice how his characters employ repetition, as in Iago's grilling of Othello in Act III, turning the Moor's words against him. And in *Ju-*

lius Caesar, as Antony emphasizes that Brutus is "an honourable man," each restatement adds new meaning to the message. As Stockton Axson notes in *Shakespeare: Thinker, Showman, and Artist,* "The same thought is repeated in many different situations through the mouths of many different characters . . . And in the very repetitions there is a suggestion of an echo of Shakespeare's own personal thoughts."

Thoughts, but also words. *Lebowski* is the ultimate example of linguistic propagation. Characters pass language back and forth, often quoting one another, and before long idiosyncratic verbiage on the order of "unchecked aggression" and "in the parlance of our time" is careening all over California. A trademark precision in word choice is on full display in *Lebowski,* with every pause, phrase, and epithet calculated in masterly style, and close attention to the text upon repeat readings only adds to our appreciation. Only a Shakespearean mind could play with words the way these characters do. Time and again, they ask each other, in effect, what the fuck they're talking about; even the subtle shifts in tone between "special lady" and "lady friend" are brought into fullest examination. *The Big Lebowski* could hardly not be Shakespearean, because it's about one of the most Shakespearean things of all: the English language.

And that's what it all comes back to: language. "Words, words, words," as the fellow said. I've loved these words. I've loved poring over the canon, discarding elements of the "bad quarto" and incorporating more accurate texts to create this, the definitive edition of *Two Gentlemen of Lebowski,* the lost work that the immortal Bard never wrote.

It's ironic, but I'm left with an authorship question of my own. I mean, I wrote it, I dig seeing my name on the cover. But I just don't think it's that simple.

Call me a receptacle, a steward, an avatar. Call me the conduit of an important idea. Maybe Shakespeare himself played muse to me, reaching down through history, flicking me on the forehead, instilling in me the strength—no, the responsibility—to finish his last work.

Or maybe I'm just a guy in a bathrobe, grasping at poetic fantasies to justify what, let's face it, could have been a complete waste of time.

That's good enough for me. It's been a great ride either way. Besides, my college reunion's coming up, and I needed something to show for the last five years besides some highlighted Folger editions and a picture of me with Anne Hathaway.

I still can't explain why I did it. Only one person ever could, and he's been dead since 1616. Shakespeare knew human nature better than anyone else; he was our finest philosopher. And only through the imaginative experience can we know his mind. So I keep reading. Searching for some kind of truth. Not just for an age, but for all time.

Lately I'm hearing a new voice woven into his words.

"Fuck it, dude," it tells me. "Let's go bowling."

That gets me through the day.

Acknowledgments

People sometimes ask me which part of *Two Gentlemen* was the most rewarding to write. This page is the answer.

I am grateful to:

Lindsay Edgecombe, my literary agent and fire warden, for unerring grace and indefatigability in shepherding my 15,000-word play and my 30,000-word e-mails.

All those at the Levine Greenberg Literary Agency who held the author's hand during this project's twisted road to publication.

Michael Szczerban, my ever-reassuring editor, for shaping a good idea into a better one.

All those at Simon & Schuster who had faith that offering me a book deal would probably not usher in the apocalypse.

Frank Cwiklik and Michele Schlossberg, for dinner in.

The New York achievers, for doing the impossible.

The goons of Something Awful, for spreading the virus.

Alyssa Milano, for upending my life in under 140 characters.

Kent Sanderson, for a phone call when I really needed one.

God, for having a sense of humor.

The fans, for obvious reasons.

And finally, my long-suffering parents, for abiding.

Illustration Credits

About the Author

Adam Bertocci is an award-winning filmmaker, screenwriter, and free-lance Bardolator working in and around New York. He is a proud graduate of the film program at Northwestern University, with a surprisingly useful minor in English literature.

A despairingly prolific creator and speedy typist, Bertocci has written and/or directed more than a dozen short films for the festival circuit. He has also written and spoken extensively on fan-created media and fan culture. *Two Gentlemen of Lebowski* is his first book and easily his best so far.

Visit him on the web at www.adambertocci.com.